ANCIENT CODE

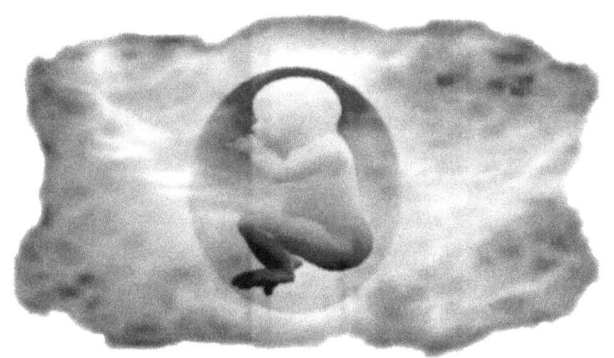

YOU are the Key to the Code

Ancient Code Copyright© 2009 by Reality Press. All rights reserved.

No part of this book may be reproduced or transmitted in any form or by any means, graphic, electronic, or mechanical, including photocopying, recording, taping or by any information storage or retrieval system, without permission in writing from the publisher at: info@reality-entertainment.com.

Reality Press
An imprint of Reality Entertainment, Inc.

For information contact:

REALITY ENTERTAINMENT
P.O. Box 91
Foresthill, CA 95631

Ph: 530-367-5389
Fx: 530-367-3024

www.reality-entertainment.com

ISBN: 978-1-934588-81-9

Printed in the United States of America.

Contents

Introduction .... *iv*
Brian Allan 1
Jack Allis 9
Kala Ambrose 15
Nick Ashron 25
Philip Coppens 33
Robert Feather 47
Philip Gardiner 53
Dr. Mitchell E. Gibson 57
Andrew Gough 73
Jasmin Gould 93
Dan Green 101
Dr. John Jay Harper 107
June-Elleni Lane 131
Janice Manning 135
Marshall Masters 143
Brian Mayne 147
Steve Mitchell 155
Nick Pope 171
Dennis Price 175
Colin Wilson 183

Introduction

By Philip Gardiner

Ancient Code the Movie is about re-connection. It is a story so old that it is shameful we humans have to keep on learning it again and again. Throughout time many have spoken out regarding the Natural world and how we as conscious humans disregard not just our place in it, but our very connection with it. Today in the twenty-first century we find ourselves in a world divided not just from our Natural state, but from each other. We have not learned that fighting one another for goods, land, prestige and power gets us nowhere. We do not see that we rape the earth for the prime material needed to cosmetically alter our shape, appearance and standing in society. Most modern scientific breakthroughs are for cosmetic purposes, not to save the starving masses that die from diseases and for whom we could discover cures. The reason is simple, the poor cannot pay. We fail utterly to see that we consistently swing vote the same people into power again and again in something we claim is democracy. We fail to see that we do have real power as a people, because more often than not we are lead like sheep.

When I wrote *Ancient Code the Movie* I wanted to get to the core of who we really are. I am not "Philip" for that is but a name; I am human, an animal, born of this world, in this solar system, in this galaxy, in this universe, indeed, from and into this Universe by the very power and energy that created it. This is no great spiritual statement, this is a statement of pure fact. And I am of the opinion that before we can proceed to empower ourselves we must come to an understanding of who we truly are.

There are many triggers and many elements on our lifelong road and there are certain things we must all come to understand if we are to be truly free of fear. These include knowledge of the true self, taking responsibility for our own actions and thoughts, understanding the pureness of love for what it is and maintaining a balance throughout our entire lives in everything we do. Three words have always spoken to me which spring from this journey – strength, will, knowledge. All three must be used in balance. To be strong can mean physical health or mental and spiritual prowess. To have will is to have a desire to cause an affect and to have knowledge is to use our strength and will effectively. Without any one of these elements we are not fully perfected. Think about it for a moment. If I will to do something and yet lack the strength to do so I will not be able to and yet if I lack the knowledge I will not know what to do. I can have the strength and the knowledge and yet lack the will and so they will be worthless. These are key, magical words that have been used for millennia by adepts across the globe who saw the truth within them.

Once we have gained an understanding of our very self and our place in the Universe – that we are not separate from it, but part of it – then we will find true love inspired within us. And that true love, regardless of lust for sex (simple evolutionary device to procreate), will be a love for life, not just for ourselves, but for those around us, for compassion will form within us. Yes, there are those such as H. G. Wells who argued for a mere evolutionary instinct - that the weakest should not survive just because the strong can support them, - but in my opinion this neglects the higher power we find when we understand our connection to Nature and the profundity of the energy we are connected to. If you ever feel that you are not special, then remember this, the energy that surges through your veins comes directly to you from the very beginning. There is no divide, no cutoff point. It is continual, it goes on, within you and your thoughts are formed via that energy. You are very special indeed. But so too are those who have been unfortunate enough to be born disabled or into the wrong "tribe." The same energy forms their thoughts too. If H. G. Wells had been right, then many so-called disabled people would not have contributed to our thoughts and lives – Hawkins is but one example. The problem comes from the fact that this same energy can be turned to the "dark side" and be used as a powerful tool to control others and after many generations it can no longer be seen for what it truly is – religion is but a single example of this. Religion may seem wonderful and have answers to our own spiritual dilemmas but are these dilemmas real in the first place? They are mainly focused around fear – the fear of loss of self. This is quite remarkable when so many people have no idea what that is in the first place and in reality it is often the fear of losing what we think we are. When we actually discover the truth, the fear dries up and does not require a controlling elite with rules and dogma to cling to.

Imagination is the most powerful element in the human being. It can imagine a good or bad future. It recreates the past. It thinks through possibilities and comes up with improvements or doomed philosophies. It is dual in nature, but if we recognize this as a fact then we have power over it. If we remember to balance the logic with the emotion and use the power of imagination, then all things are possible.

The following chapters are brought to you because we imagined the possibilities of a book such as this. The power of that thought spread to the insightful people who participated and they have brought the power of their imagination to this work, for us all. I hope you enjoy the book and the film and that you too spread the power.

The Sirens are Sounding
A short polemic on a doomed culture

By Brian Allan © 2009

Author's Note

There are many indicators presaging the spiritual collapse of any given society and by extension any civilization and, worryingly, many of them are already here in plain sight: let's consider two brief snapshots of the same event, a recent murder in the UK and what this might represent in microcosm. Any society that is afraid to criticise or rail against that which is demonstrably wrong is not a free society.

Click

Anger, selfishness and fear: in 2008, in England, a young man, Jimmy Mizen aged 16, was murdered for no better reason than he was in the wrong place at the wrong time. His murderer, a youth named Jake Fahri, 19, was already known to the police as a heavy cannabis user and school dropout who had previously been cautioned for causing trouble with the Mizen family. He murdered Jimmy following a scuffle in a bakers shop by throwing a glass dish at him, a fragment of which severed an artery in Jimmy's neck. Jimmy bled to death in his brother's arms on the floor of the shop. After Fahri's conviction Jimmy's father, in a statement to the public, said that, "We have become a country of anger, selfishness and fear."

Click

The murderer, Jake Fahri, as he was led from the dock called out to his weeping mother that she should not worry as he would be "all right." Sadly he was speaking no more than the truth, something that is a searing indictment on how society and the law treats murderers, psychopaths, pedophiles, rapists and suspected terrorists. He will indeed be "all right," condemned to a life of relative ease paid for out of the public purse funded by the taxes of decent, hard working people. The same decent people who are faced with continually rising bills for goods and services they strive to pay for; of course he will be "all right." All this while the banks and other financial institutions crash and tumble round our ears, and those who ran these former organs of rectitude and probity break cover and run for the hills clutching the rich pickings made from the reckless buccaneering deals they drove through, again with the full knowledge and acquiescence of national governments. Anger, selfishness and fear … and greed?

The Sirens are Sounding

"Anger, selfishness and fear," the heartfelt cry of a sorely grieving father and a few words that should carry the chilly wind of uncomfortable truth into the public psyche. Perhaps added to those comments should have been lack of shame, a complete abrogation of personal responsibility, greed, hopelessness and despair. All howls of pain against the onset of lawlessness and its inevitable cure; the imposition of an oppressive police state in the name of restoring the rule of law and order; an accident or is it something else? Society has, in the main, been actively encouraged to lose its sense of shame and self worth, two vital ingredients in the glue that bound it together. This, the glue that gave us a sense of decency, has been deliberately weakened, diluted and debased by an insidious and lazy media driven form of glib "vox pop" culture cynically fanned by the ever-growing mountain of glossy magazines designed to promote a culture of near vacuous celebrity as a lifestyle worth aspiring to. Anger, **selfishness and fear.**

It matters not whether these magazines and tabloid newspapers can justify the near deification of, in some cases, near illiterate individuals whose sole claim to fame is due to their good fortune to inherit, earn by whatever means, or simply marry into money and fame. All that matters is the promotion of a lifestyle that cannot be achieved by those who aspire to the premise of style over substance at all costs, why? What is truly terrifying is the automatic assumption by a gullible public who dote on these magazines and those who (dis)grace their pages, that the opinions expressed by the so called "celebrities" are their own words and that the majority of them are possessed of a modicum of worthwhile intellect. One has only to consider the flurry of "autobiographies" that appear as any particular media star is in the ascendant, these so-called autobiographies are not written by those whose life is offered for public inspection, they are ghost-written by others infinitely more qualified to do so. This is a position that has been eagerly encouraged by the manipulators, those whose lives are lived in the shadows, those who try to divert attention from their own agendas by promising the moon while delivering only hate and division to further sunder an already weakened society. *Anger,* **selfishness** *and fear.*

Another insidious factor introduced by those who promote this consciousness numbing agenda is that positive criticism must be suppressed by any and all means possible, especially if they can convince the masses that it is in some way wrong to consider alternatives contradictory to their own inward looking views. This is of course quite right, because from their point of view the values that protected society for millennia are an inconvenience that has been increasingly swept away in the headlong rush to modernise, liberalize, debase, uproot and destroy tradition and thereby allow the slow and insidious poison of totalitarian control to take root. However, there is an answer, it is not difficult nor does it require a great deal of courage and it lies within the gift of each and every one of us; consider this.

It is not wrong to question unfairness, it is not wrong to ask why the workshy and feckless are rewarded for their instinctive nihilism. Nor, in particular, is it wrong to question the social services concerning the safety of infants left in the care of frequently addicted, and supremely unsuitable parents whose dependency culture based lifestyles are, at best, chaotic. In this last instance the worst one can receive is the disapproval of officialdom, while the best is the knowledge that you may have prevented a childhood of unimaginable suffering and in some cases the death of an innocent. In addition it is not wrong to argue against and reject overt obscenity hidden under the thin and tired masquerade of art, nor is it wrong to protect society from the increasing and ever younger cynical sexualisation and exploitation of youth in the name of profit and so called "progress." All this with the tactic approval of parents too entrapped and enmeshed in a system where they were too preoccupied with their own concerns to see it encroaching upon them. Profit and progress, the two watchwords of an increasingly ailing society, just how far do either of these concepts have to continue until they become unacceptable by any decent standards? However and woefully, these are now seen as positive values that hold sway and are actively encouraged in our modern society.

Is anyone really surprised when they see another bloody outrage occur in the world, they occur in the name of whatever extremist organization feels sufficiently courageous or marginalized enough to launch their cowardly attacks, again on the innocent and defenceless? But are they courageous, are they marginalized, are they ignored until they feel they have no other choice, or is there a much deeper and infinitely more malign agenda afoot? What we see on an almost daily basis are continuing examples of creeping state control, whether this takes the form of tasers or pepper and CS sprays being issued to the police (in the UK). Indeed, we now have new and improved tasers that are wireless and no longer hard-wired to their launchers. Instead, the officer presses the trigger, launches the barbed dart and activates the firing circuit by wireless remote control, refinement indeed!

Money for these purchases is invariably found in the public purse. Why? To protect 'A' the officer and 'B', the public, is the stock answer. How long then until all police officers are routinely armed with firearms rather than depending on trained fast response units. All of this long after legally owned hand guns were removed from private ownership in the wake of the Dunblane massacre, the instigator of which, Thomas Hamilton, conveniently killed himself with one of his own weapons. Was Hamilton an unwitting and/or controlled asset? This is something else we will probably never know. Handguns and their proscription were the measure used to further undermine society, a "quick fix," fanned by an understandable revulsion to find the culprits, which in this case were, by proxy, the owners of legal handguns. Might this however been something else, testing the water to discover what they could "sell;" to the public so to speak?

Never forget that the public, in Europe at least, has had ever more stringent rules regarding the possession of firearms foisted upon them in the wake of the Russian revolution and the murder of Czar Nicholas and his family. This was something that might well have found a common resonance throughout the royal house of Europe and, in particular, the United Kingdom where the division between the have and have not's was greatest. Incidentally, since the removal of private handguns from the UK, the number of gun related incidents and deaths remorselessly increase year on year, the removal of handguns did not stop this, but it was never intended to. ***Anger,*** *selfishness **and fear.***

Another manifest symptom is the increasing proliferation of video cameras, for the safety of all we are told, but as ever they are a double-edged weapon against both society and the criminals that prey on it. "No problem" say the apologists, "no need to worry" they insist, "if you've done nothing you have nothing to fear;" really, "nothing to fear?" Yes, sadly there is, there is a great deal to fear, fear for individual freedoms in the context of a perceived need for protection, protection from what exactly, from lawless elements in society, from terrorist threats, or from the very government that is elected to maintain public safety? Well, yes and no, there is nothing to fear from the elected governments who only pursue their own short term agendas, the fear emanates from and is created by the unchanging and embedded permanent government hidden in the recesses of the so called "civil service."

Here are the inscrutable mandarins who actually run the country, this is extremely convenient for them, governments are only the masks that can be discarded and replaced as required, but the real grasp on power never changes. Oddly enough an almost exact parallel exists within the hallowed walls of The Vatican, but in reverse. Depending on which Pope is enthroned, his political views are reflected in the power and influence wielded by either the Jesuits or, much more recently, "Opus Dei," (lit. Gods Work). The more right wing and conservative the Pope, the more this suits Opus Dei, and the more left wing the Pope the more the Jesuits benefit. Any "hung papacy," should such a concept be possible, would be courted avidly by both of these special interest groups for their own benefit. (*Anger, **selfishness and fear***).

Anger, selfishness and fear, again the same three unchanging, permeable, simple and unambiguous words, represent all too human feelings and emotions. However, in addition to being the visible symptoms they are also extremely effective levers of control. A society that is angry at itself for its own sins of omission, a society beset with self-interest, greed and material possessions. Sadly, this is also a society too dumbstruck and petrified with fear invented by successive governments to speak out against the patent abuses against the natural laws of common decency and fair play carried out as it watches, squirming with self-loathing and impotence.

This is a society and indeed an entire culture that is divided and can easily be manipulated. But even on the brink it is not too late, we can still take society back, we can still strike out against the black flag of oppression that slowly rises above us, but it will not be easy, far from it. One of the first props holding it in place is the sick culture of political correctness, an insidious and increasingly pervasive culture that demonizes common sense and truth. It happens because society as a whole allows it to happen and for no other reason it is the creation of an increasing intelligentsia that found a safe haven in the hidden courts of the civil service where it could dream up and enforce pointless rules and regulation predicated on some notional improvement in public protocols of behavior. (*Anger, selfishness and fear*).

Although, as already alluded to, the road would not be easy, the method is astonishingly simple, just say NO the next time a fresh piece of stupid and pointless legislation is proposed, something that was created to justify the job of some low grade, faceless and self-serving politician or bureaucrat. Simple acts of defiance that can and would spread, take back the person, take back the town, take back the country, take back the world. **Love, Generosity and courage.**

# # #

Brian Allan is a lifelong researcher into the mysteries and contradictions posed by paranormal phenomena and has devoted his life to seeking answers to some of these anomalies. This has involved him in a series of "hands on" investigations encompassing everything from poltergeist infestations, hauntings and spirit possession to claims of alien abduction. From this solid groundwork he has developed a reputation as a speaker and presenter at various conferences across the length and breadth of the United Kingdom. This in turn developed into Brian acting as an adviser and participant in various international TV and radio broadcasts involving almost all aspects of the paranormal.

Following years of active investigations, which allowed truly amazing glimpses and encounters with things normally hidden for view, Brian began specializing in the esoteric aspects of Rosslyn Chapel and in 2005, along with a small, hand selected team, he was permitted to test some of his theories involving specific sonic frequencies within its enigmatic structure. This in turn lead to the discovery of an area inside the Chapel which Brian is convinced is a still active "portal" leading to what may be a store of forbidden knowledge.

Never one to rest on his laurels, Brian decided to commit some of his cases and the fascinating research that they required to paper in a series of books. Much of what Brian writes about reveals that there are a number of fundamental and immutable truths governing the nature of what we perceive around us and that we live in a multiverse inhabited by beings utterly unlike the human race. In Brian's books we also discover that magic is a technology like any other and that quantum physics may hold the secrets to this most arcane of subjects.

Brian and Ann Allan (paranormal investigators) website www.p-e-g.co.uk

Connecting with the Divine Spirit with Our Vibration

By Jack Allis

*Connecting with the divine spirit
of a living universe with our vibration.*

This is how I begin my presentation and DVD, which both have the same title, *2012 the Shift – Transforming Challenges into Blessings*. And I assure you it's the most important thing you will hear me say.

This is after I have created a sacred space by singing a chant, while playing my magical shakers from Paraguay. Even though the audience doesn't know the words, they almost always join in. The words don't matter anyway. It's all about the vibration.

After I say this, I pause, and look deeply into the eyes of my audience.

Invariably, they are with me – their eyes plugged into mine – and plugged into the wondrous moment we have created together. Their energy and mine are one.

After savoring the moment, I repeat: *connecting with the divine spirit of a living universe with our vibration.*

I take another moment to let it percolate some more, and I continue:

This is the primary source of our protection, in these times of monumental Earth changes and paradigm shifts, and the primary source of our power to create the new world of light and spirit.

On the topic of 2012 & the Great Shift of the Ages, this is really all people need to hear. With a topic this vast, and potentially complex, it is vitally important to keep things as simple and uncomplicated as possible. This is the essence of all true spirituality anyway – simplicity – so simple that little children understand it without even trying. It is also the essence of virtually all the ancient prophecies, from indigenous cultures spanning the globe, dating back tens of thousands of years, and sometimes far longer. This includes the Egyptians, the Mayans, the Incas, numerous tribes in South America and Africa, the Hopi, and virtually every other Native American tribe.

These are sources that are far more trustworthy than mainstream, civilized sources because they have retained their connection with the one true source of higher consciousness and spiritual knowledge, and that is their intimate relationship and love affair with the natural world. The old paradigm is unsustainable, and is collapsing, as it must, because this is precisely the connection the western, civilized world has lost. It has lost the connection with life's vital energy, and with the rhythm and flow of life, and fallen into the fatal trap of placing its primary emphasis on the material world, at the expense of the spiritual.

These ancient indigenous cultures, at least the ones that weren't contaminated or destroyed totally by Western Civilization, never lost their intimate connection with the natural world. Their keen observations of natural cycles allowed them to become expert astronomers, scientists and cosmologists, as well as sorcerers and magicians, who were capable of stupendous feats that apparently violated the rules of ordinary, linear, cause and effect reality.

And as far as the shift is concerned, and this extraordinary time we are now living in, these prophecies all had the same basic message for us. Here it is, in my words.

Yes, this is a time of colossal Earth changes and paradigm shifts. It is the completion of a 26,000 year galactic cycle, in which the old world, one of materiality and the attempt to control the forces of nature, will collapse, and there will be an opportunity to create an entirely new world, one that is governed by the spirit. Winter Solstice 2012 is a key date in virtually all of these prophecies. This also is the date the Mayan Calendar ended. However, beware of placing excessive importance on this, or any other, specific date, as most of the prophecies point to this time in general, and portray the shift as more of a gradual process, taking place in a window of time around 12/21/12, as opposed to one dramatic point. We have no definitive way of knowing how large this window of time is, but at the time of this writing (July 2009), it is clearly obvious that "the shift" has already started. "The shift" is happening, and it's happening NOW!

However, "the shift" is not going to just happen by itself. It's up to the human beings of the planet Earth to make it happen. And there's only one way to do this, and that is with the power of our higher consciousness and spirituality. This process of potential transformation is one of ascension – ascension from heavy to light - from higher density to lower density – from lower frequency to higher frequency. And these Earth changes and these paradigm shifts will be a monumental challenge for us, the inhabitants of the planet. This has happened before, and these changes were colossal in nature, and probably will be again. These Earth changes include the possibility of the reversal of the Earth's magnetic poles and its rotation, several days of total darkness (or light), great floods, intense winds, greatly increased earthquake and volcanic activity, and the disappearance of land masses and emergence of others – the equivalent of a massive face lift or cleansing. Please take special note of the use of the term "possibility" in relationship to these Earth changes, as none of this is etched in stone. We are clearly in uncharted territory here.

The prophecies also agree that those human beings who are not prepared, and who don't have their act together energetically and spiritually, could be in for a very rough ride, possibly ending in the extinction of the entire species. But again, it's up to us. The fate of the planet rests in our hands, and it is clear what we are called upon to do.

To call this story the most important of our time is a silly understatement. And simplicity here, again, is so vitally important because few topics have been as needlessly complicated and confused as the shift, invariably resulting in stimulating fear of hysterical levels, and catastrophic visions of doomsday scenarios, which was not the intent of the prophecies. As glorious as the Internet revolution has been in giving masses of people exposure to this vast frontier of unfiltered information, it also has its flip side. Sometimes too much can be too much, when any zealot or nut case has equal access to this medium, and can use it to get their message out there.

The same principle applies for what are known as disinformants. There are those among us, usually in positions of power, whose true agenda is not the spiritual fulfillment and liberation of the human race, but rather its suppression and enslavement. I will be referring to them as the dark side. The Internet is a perfect medium for the dark side to disseminate false information (disinformation, propaganda, brainwashing), the purpose of which is to confuse the issues, and knock people off the track of truth, with the objective of enhancing their power over them. Not everybody is who they say they are, and disinformants are rampant throughout our world, and sadly, this is painfully true in such ostensibly benevolent movements as the New Age and the greens.

All of which means it is incumbent on each of us to be aware of this, to filter through this vast sea of information with due diligence, and to decide what is right and wrong for us. Things are never as complicated, or terrifying, as they are usually made out to be. A good standard rule is: if it's too complicated, or if it doesn't feel good, look somewhere else.

Connecting with the divine spirit of a living universe with our vibration. This is the primary source of our protection and our power.

It sounds nice and sweet and simple to me, but perhaps to some, this might sound vague or esoteric. And it really isn't.

We are not just our physical bodies. We are our totality – body, mind and spirit. As the Mexican Indian sorcerer, don Juan, from the writings of Carlos Castaneda, says: we are luminous beings. In altered states of consciousness, the sorcerers of don Juan's lineage saw humans as egg-shaped clusters of luminous fibers, which had awareness, and which were connected to all the energy surrounding them in the entire universe, like a gigantic spider web of luminosity. This energetic view of the world was confirmed by quantum science, which discovered a world, where everything, in its essence, was interconnected energy, which was governed by an unseen intelligence of some kind. This, of course, is the essence of true spirituality.

Like all energy, we have a vibration, a frequency. And there is a direct relationship between our energetic vibration and our emotions and thoughts.

Emotions and thoughts are, actually, energy flowing through the pathways of our physical body, and beyond. And there is unanimous agreement among every spiritual tradition worth its salt, from everywhere on the planet, past and present, that human beings are at their spiritual peak when they experience life with certain feelings and thoughts. Specifically, these feelings are feelings of relaxation, peacefulness, joy and love. And these thoughts are reflections of these feelings, springing from a mind that is quiet and still, and that sees the brilliance of the world.

When we experience life in this peak spiritual state, this puts us in alignment or resonance with the divine spirit of a living universe, the source of all creation. This is what it means to be in the rhythm and flow of life, and in harmony with the forces of the natural world, which is the same as being in resonance with divine law. This is when our spiritual power is at its maximum. And this vibrational connection is the one true source of manifesting what we want in life. Everything, ultimately, springs from our connection with spirit.

In order to create the new world, it is necessary for us to make this energetic and spiritual connection both as individuals, and in mass, which is referred to as critical mass. Critical mass is the energetic point, at which a sufficient number of human beings have retained this connection, where amazing and unprecedented things will start to happen. Like the 100th monkey, once enough of us reconnect with our spiritual power, we become a force that cannot be stopped, and we won't need crumbling political, economic, religious and social structures to help. No thank you – we can handle it on our own. As David Rhodes, one of the heroes of my novel, *Infinity's Flower*, says: "If we are in tune with the Earth, and if we are in tune with the divine spirit, then the Earth and the divine spirit will shower us with unimaginable blessings." This is the source of our protection and power in the face of this challenge, or any other, and that's all we need.

#

Jack Allis is the author of *Infinity's Flower - A Tale of 2012 & the Great Shift of the Ages*. Since its publication in September 2007, he has become the living embodiment of its message, traveling the country, and delivering it to as many awakening souls as he can reach. He has written two other novels, *Infinity's Children* and *Masters of Destiny*, and is currently working on a new book

2012 & the Shift – Transforming Challenges into Blessings as well as his popular monthly e-newsletter. In addition to his writing, Jack is also a personal growth and spiritual teacher, working with people in person, by telephone, and over the Internet. In his teaching work, Jack emphasizes the harmony of the body, mind and spirit, and he teaches people how to experience peacefulness and joy in their lives by reconnecting with life's vital energy and with the rhythm and flow of life. For more information, please visit www.jackallis.com.

The Rise and Return of the Divine Feminine (Three Become One)

By Kala Ambrose

Alone on the mountaintop, the old woman carefully lowers her body down onto her prayer blanket making herself comfortable. It is still dark outside and while the moonlight served to guide her way along the narrow path, she didn't find it necessary. She instinctively knew where she was going and what it would look like when she reached the summit. Preparing herself, she pulled her shawl closer around her and waited. There in the distance, came the first glimmer of light, the first breaking of dawn. This was a day she had waited centuries for, as she had spent each lifetime studying ancient secrets and following clues. Each painstaking step and lifetime through good and bad, she was born again into a new culture, as a priestess, druid, warrior, witch and healer. All these lifetimes of experience and now it was coming down to this moment, and still she was unsure what exactly would occur, she only knew that this was the time and place and that it was unfolding exactly as it should.

As the light of the sun began to rise over the ridge of the mountain, a solar flare from the sun sparked, illuminating an emerald green ray, which arched over the mountaintop. This ray had traveled from the heart of the Milky Way Galaxy, a gift from the galactic mother, ushering in a new age on this day of December 21, 2012, the Winter Solstice.

Moving over the mountain, the green ray burst into sparks of light washing over the old woman. The tiny rays entered through her skin, filling her heart with a warm glow. The sun was rising steadily now and lower down on the mountain, the old woman could hear villagers and monks who were celebrating and greeting the sun, their voices reverberating in a chant accompanied by the sound of a gong.

The arc of sunlight moved closer to the woman highlighting the deep green trees and grass in the valley below. Following the direction of the stream of light, the woman observed on the ground below what appeared to be a figure emerging from the trees. To her surprise, it was a young girl with long red hair and she was moving in the direction of the old woman. The girl ran following the ray of the sun. She appeared to be under no stress and her focus was intent on the direction she was heading. As she drew closer to the woman, she caught the old woman's eyes, startling her with their intensity. Locking eyes now with the woman, the young girl did not drop her gaze and held her eyes steadfast as she moved closer towards her. The old woman studied the girl with great interest and held her gaze in return. The girl was oddly familiar and she felt no concern as the girl continued to run towards her following the path of light created by the sun. Keeping her eyes locked on the young girl, the old woman stood up slowly and opened her arms outward, to welcome the girl to approach her. While there was no need, as the child was heading directly for her, it was an act of reverence and acceptance.

The girl was close now and her body began to shimmer, transforming. It was nothing like the old woman had ever seen before, the girl appeared in one moment to be a third dimensional flesh and blood child, and in the next moment her body would alter into a form of light and then she would shimmer back into a girl. Fascinated, the woman held her ground and waited to see what would happen next. The girl was within speaking distance now, but no sound came from either of them. She continued to approach the old woman never breaking her run, and her body began to transform again as she approached the woman. The sunlight was fully on her body, highlighting her red hair, giving the appearance that her entire head was crowned in a brilliant light. Each time she shimmered, her physical form altered. The girl was growing taller and she now looked to be around eighteen. Shimmering again, she now appeared to be in her early '20s, her body continuing to lengthen and grow. Now within 15 feet of the old woman, the girl transformed again into a woman in her late '20s. The light of the sun covered them both and the old woman squinted through the light to see the young woman. To her surprise, the redheaded woman had picked up speed and was heading directly for her, with no intent it appeared of stopping.

As the sun fully illuminated the old woman, she lifted her head skyward and the message she had waited lifetimes to receive entered into her consciousness. Opening her eyes, she looked back at the girl. Digging her heels into the ground to steady her body, she opened her arms just as the young woman ran directly into her making full contact.

Upon the collision and impact, the two bodies melded together, lifting the two women into the air as the rays of the Sun encapsulated around them. The two women surrendered to the energy, as the rays of light drew closer around them forming a sacred pattern, which began to fluctuate in color and speed. Down in the valley below, several of the villagers along with the monks stopped to watch this display on the mountain above them, which they would later describe as a Merkaba of light floating over the valley. Its brilliance was not only dazzling to see, but the sound of musical chords could be heard as the light display began to float down the mountain towards them.

The Merkaba of light held the two women, who could no longer be seen clearly in the energy field. As the capsule floated closer to the valley, the light pattern began to slow its pace. Lowering itself to just a few inches over the ground, the villagers watched from a careful distance as the light and sound patterns dissipated and a naked woman dropped from the light onto the grass. The woman rested quietly on the grass, her breathing moving rapidly as the last bits of light moved away from her body. Her pale skin contrasted in the light with her red hair and as she stood up to face the villagers and monks, they could see green light emanating from her skin, glowing brightest around her heart. Not saying a word, she held her arms in the air, embracing the light as the green rays of light were now entering the area where the monks and villagers now stood.

Without further time to consider where this woman had come from, the rays of light hit each person in the village, lifting their bodies slightly off the ground as the rays entered their bodies. The woman observed the light now emitting from each of their souls. The spark was ignited now in each soul with the wisdom of the ancient ones. The dawn of the new age and the next evolution of humanity had begun. Humanity would now begin to evolve into a balance of the divine masculine and divine feminine within each person, and they would discover the balance of the heart and the mind with the soul.

Grounding to the earth, she watched the rays depart along with the sun as they shifted to the west, to spread this energy with others around the earth. Becoming aware of her body, she realized that she had no idea where she was on earth. In what had appeared to be only a few short moments ago, she had been with family and friends in Hawaii, preparing to celebrate winter solstice 2012. She had been in a deep meditation where she had seen a vision of herself as a young girl in the sunlight, running with full abandon and joy. Then she saw the old woman and recognized that it was herself in the future. The vision shifted and she was back viewing herself as a young girl and saw through her own eyes as the young girl locked eyes with the old woman as they both moved towards her. She had felt the body of the young girl as it collided and melded into the old woman's and felt herself being pulled into the light with them. Then there was a period of floating, in a sea of energy and love and that place that she had gone to years before, when beings from the other side had released her from her body and took her into their plane of existence. It had been so lovely, basking in an energy field of bliss. With a rush of wind and light, the three women became one and the next thing she knew, she was naked, laying on the grass in front of a group of people, some that she could identify from their robes as monks. The last thing she remembered before being lowered to the ground by the light, were these words… "We have shifted into the new time, beginning now, no longer are bodies caught in the past or future, it is only now." And so was she. She was now connected and remembered fully all of her past lives and the experiences she had gained over the years. The ancient wisdom was within her and her connection as a high priestess with the goddess and all it represented was fully activated in her cellular memory and energy fields. In this moment, she had been reborn as her name given at birth had prophesized: Time Reborn.

* * *

This vision first came to me as a recurring dream when I was about the age of six. Being born with psychic abilities, I had dreams I could recall since childhood and on most nights, I remembered at least three dreams a night, an occurrence which still continues till this day. As a child, what I remembered most vividly about this dream, was how it felt to run on the grass with the light shining above me. It was the most fascinating feeling, as there was no exertion as I ran, nor any sense of urgency. It was very similar to my favorite activity at the time, dancing, which always gave me the feeling that I was floating slightly above the ground, moving to a rhythm much older and more powerful than me. In the dreams as I moved closer to the old woman, I would experience a feeling of becoming lighter in every aspect. My body and thoughts were relaxed and I felt no fear as the light illuminated my path. Before I awoke each time in the dream I would hear these words spoken aloud by a woman I could not see ... "We are all One, One Energy, from One Light. Let us band together as humans, with love for all of humanity, living each day in harmony as we explore our spirit."

I continued to have the recurring dream until the age of 13. It returned in my late twenties, after a long period of time where I had pushed my emotions and my psychic ability down deep inside of me. As I went through a period of re-awakening and connecting with my spiritual self, these memories floated back up into the surface along with the psychic abilities I had tried to ignore, the auric fields I had closed my eyes to and the guides and other beings returned, whom I had been so close to in childhood, that I made sure to make space in my bed for them every night, in case they wanted to sleep next to me. The dreams returned, nightly, though I had never really been able to get them to stop completely, no matter how hard I had tried. This particular dream came again; only this time I was the old woman. I saw my life as I taught the ancient wisdom teachings, along with where I lived and worked and those who came to study with me. I connected with the energy of the old wise woman and the wisdom and power that resided in her heart and body. One morning after awakening from this dream, my heart chakra opened. During this time, I experienced what is described as the dark night of the soul. I felt the energy from all that I had created with my thoughts, words, actions and deeds in this lifetime and how my actions had affected each person I had encountered, both positive and negative. During this painful and overwhelming ordeal, the woman spoke to me gently this time, comforting me with her presence. Softly she would say, "It is time to connect with the loving Spirit, the secrets are meant to be shared." Once I completed this life-altering journey, the dream of the light and the young girl and old woman dissipated again.

As we approach the Winter Solstice of 2012, the dream is occurring again and I now connect with the woman from the light capsule, who is reborn with the gifts of what the young girl and the old woman worked to bring to me at this moment in time. When I awake from the dream now, my soul speaks these words, which have become the code that I live by ... "Spirit does not exist in just one location; rather it is all encompassing, living within and amongst us in each moment, thought and action. I believe that Spirit is raised to its highest level, when individuals gather with wisdom, compassion and a discerning desire to provide service to humanity."

As 2012 grows near, my work continues sharing the ancient esoteric teachings and working in service to humanity as we prepare to enter the new age. In my work I connect with spirit guides and other beings of light. One of the questions that I have asked them recently regarding 2012 is this … Why are psychics having a difficult time seeing time lines in the future for the people they are reading for and for the world as 2012 approaches? It was explained to me that what we understand as time, is changing very quickly. What used to take years, even decades to occur, now takes only days and months. Because time is shifting so rapidly, we now have the greatest potential to create with our thoughts. Time as we know and understand it, is changing and soon will not be relevant to the way we will live.

I have also asked, why have many of the prophecies predicted for this time, not come true? The prophecies I speak of are of the darkest times for humanity, which many describe as the entire world suffering, starving and in pain. While certainly we are experiencing troubled times, it is not as bad as predicted. As it was explained to me, we have a destiny, but we also have free will. As part of our destiny, humanity evolves with each new age. With each shift, as in any change, there is great fear and resistance to change, which causes the darkest of times as people react in fear. Humanity is destined to enter this next age, moving out of the period of Kali Yuga as the Hindus describe it, and moving into the Age of Aquarius, as mystics would describe. This shift is our destiny; however how we choose to react to the changes is our free will. The world is evolving and altering on a minute-by-minute basis and with this many of the veils are lifting, not just from between the planes, but also within each person. Ancient secrets tucked away deep within each soul are now being activated again within our consciousness. As I write in my book, "*9 Life Altering Lessons: Secrets of the Mystery Schools Unveiled*," the wisdom from the ancient teachings were protected by implanting them into our deep subconscious until we were ready again to enter the temple and receive the illumination within. This ancient wisdom was hidden within each of us and as we enter into this new age, the code is being revealed. We are opening it to reveal the ancient secrets and mysteries. One of the first secrets decoded was the knowledge that we are creators and as such, we can manifest with our thoughts and desires.

As people began to awaken, a hush and a prayer were shared by the ancient beings as they watched and waited. Their concern being, would those who cracked the first code, use this rediscovered ability only to manifest their personal desires? Or would they think beyond the material world of how they could give unselfishly to others? Like all children with a new toy, some time was expected where each soul would play with this new gift, testing it out to see how it works. There have been a few tense moments, for it was decreed long ago that when the first code was revealed and humanity understood that what you think, you can change and/or create, that this would also coincide with the shift of the ages and time imploding on itself, which would supercharge the energy of what each person was manifesting. Because of this explosive and empowering gift, it became virtually impossible for psychics to see a time line too far into the future when reading for a person. In the past, what the person was thinking or drawing towards them, would take years to create, and the psychic could view this outcome in the energetic fields around the body. Now with time and energy shifting constantly, the future outcome of what a person desires, can literally change in days. As my guides explained, The power of free will, now enhanced with the first key to the code and the super charged movement of time, has created a literal "free will free-for-all."

Returning back to my original question to my guides, as to why we are not in the darkest of times, which had been prophesized, it was explained to me that this had shifted because of free will. No one could be entirely sure if enough souls here on earth would awaken to receive the first code and then move beyond selfish means to help humanity through this evolution. To the immense joy of the other side, a great number of souls were willing to sacrifice and move beyond personal desires and dedicated themselves to help others, help the world, and in the process, save themselves and everyone along with them. This has been an ongoing process, building over centuries, with some of the brighter moments recently being the peace movement in the '60s, the harmonic convergence in the '80s, and what is to come after 2012. The higher love energy of many souls here on earth, has served to remove some of the fear involved with making this change. Because of this sacrifice, even what Nostradamus foresaw has altered, due to this true "shift in consciousness."

The greatest gift one can offer to the world at this time is to focus on thoughts of peace and love. Humanity is awakening to the fact that we are all one and looking at the earth and how to care for it, learning to be a steward of the earth and understanding that the ways of living in greed and disconnection with each other and the earth are shattering. Old karmic patterns and karma itself is being released now as we leave the age of Kali Yuga and move into the new age.

The destruction of old patterns, along with time speeding up, has opened a new thought wave which is altering our perception of reality every day and will continue to do so through 2012 and beyond. The time continuum is being altered. Truly, we are living in a new age, where what we think, we attract in a very rapid fashion, both positive and negative and this is being activated on a grand scale.

As a soul who chose to return to the earth plane during this very important time in the evolution in humanity, do you remember who you are? Do you remember that you are a magnificent creation of the universe, which has spent eons building and working to come to this point in time to create this golden age. You have a divine right and inheritance and you are standing waist deep in an ocean of transformational energy. Crystal clear waters are swirling around you and with a few words and a wave of your wand, these waters will stand at attention following your every move, heeding your call!

You have been conditioned over the years to forget and ignore the most important lessons in life, presented in fantasies, fairy tales and mythologies. For many, the veil was closed, weighed down in adulthood with tales of economic woes and perceived dangers lurking around every corner. What happened to the days of childhood when you laughed in the face of danger, brandishing a sword to protect and guide you? Dear ones, I tell you now, that we have been put under a spell, a "Spell of Entrapment" and the time has come to break the spell.

To break the spell you have been placed under, hold your arms in the air and repeat this aloud three times:

"I AM a Divine Being Of Light, and I Welcome and Receive All of the Universal Gifts to Which Are My Divine Right and Are For My Highest and Best!"

Do you feel the rush of energy coming to you now? 2012 is near and it is your time to awaken into this new age of which we are about to receive. Generous souls have been working on the earth and other planes to rouse you from your slumber so that you can awaken now and receive your inheritance. Have no fear, as you do not walk alone. Many stand ready to be of service to guide you on your journey. Great wizards and wise women are rallying the call, sharing the teachings of the ancient ways, easing these thoughts back into the sea of consciousness to rise forth once again.

Awaken now magnificent soul, to your divine state of being, the state of an open mind and loving heart. Do you remember that happiness is a state of mind? You knew this as a child, you chose to be happy and therefore you were, regardless of circumstances. Live in this state of grace with the eyes of a child, where each moment is bursting with opportunity with time to play and explore! In this stream of consciousness, you are open to the good surrounding you and you are able to take advantage of each opportunity flowing in your direction. Enhance and strengthen your positive thoughts, directing the flow in the direction of your dreams, but never forget, you already have inherited and live in the perpetual state and ocean of abundance.

And there we are gentle readers and here we stand with your splendid magnanimous souls on display, radiating light and power. Stand tall, this is your time, set sail on the energy ocean surrounding you and discover new lands. Do you remember? Can you crack the code? Are you ready to awaken and connect with the secrets hidden in your soul? Do you still believe in fairy tales? I do and this one is ready and waiting, your new adventure awaits you!

For the next key to the code, follow this clue: "To Thine Own Self Be True."

#

Kala Ambrose is the author of *9 Life Altering Lessons: Secrets of the Mystery Schools Unveiled* and host of metaphysical talk radio - *The Explore Your Spirit with Kala Show* www.ExploreYourSpirit.com   Kala teaches esoteric wisdom from the mystery schools of ancient Egypt and Greece and lectures on Business Intuition, Auras and Chakras, Dream Vision/Work, and The Return of the Divine Feminine.

The Ancient Code: Man and Nature

By Nick Ashron

The Ancient Code highlights the interconnectedness between Man and Nature.

This is something that I have felt from a small child spending most of my time contentedly sitting in trees just feeling at "one" with these ancient beings. At the age of 8 years old I saw a TV documentary with a Native American Elder speaking of his love and gratitude for the abundance that Nature brings forth and how he honored the Earth. This struck a resonant chord within me and I have felt an affinity with Native American Spirituality ever since.

Other cultures such as Aborigines also pay homage and gratitude to the Earth and Nature and are so in tune with the natural environment that they even feel they are guided by the consciousness of the Earth to find water in the seemingly most sparse desert areas. Most of these tribal cultures have always believed that "Man" is the caretaker of the Earth. Unfortunately western man has not honored this concept at all and has in fact been doing the opposite – raping the Earth for its natural resources without any concern for the consequences.

In my understanding the Earth is a living conscious being and we can therefore "tune in" to that consciousness by choosing to be a loving and harmonious benevolent energy walking this Earth, paying our respect, honoring "her" and being in gratitude for the sustenance "she" brings forth. Appreciation of "her" grandeur and the variety of species – from plants to animals – goes a long way to maintaining harmony here on the Earth, as one of the universal laws is cause and effect. So what we hand out we get back. A negative cause will have a negative effect and a positive thought will bring about a positive effect. This, to the best of my ability, is why I choose to be a positive energy in the world.

When I was younger many of my friends would go on protest marches being very "anti" in their outlook and approach to things they did not like in society. Whilst I totally understood their viewpoints I could not advocate the immense negativity, anger and destructive attitudes and behaviors that these individuals portrayed. In my simplistic thinking I have always thought the best way to counter something that is negative is to do something positive on the basis that everything in the universe is energy when broken down to its basic level. Therefore if you had a pair of scales and placed a negative energy on one side, it would tip one way. To get angry, negative and even violent over some issues, even though you may feel justified or have the best intent, just tips the scales to the negative energy side even more. To do something positive and loving even though it may appear to be completely disassociated with the issue at hand, is still a positive energy and it can then start to balance the scales in a positive direction. This concept just seemed logical to me when I first started to embark on my own personal spiritual journey and was presented with concepts that were new to me. I would always break them down to their simplest level of understanding and then if I could not find a practical application to that concept or idea that could enhance my everyday moment of here and now, then it would just be a load of "talk" in spite of how interesting it might seem.

Having been on my spiritual pathway now for over 30 years, it has been revealed to me that the most profound spiritual truths are actually very simple, though not necessarily easy to put into practice due to the immense amount of negative conditioning and dare I say "brain-washing" that humanity has been subjected to for thousands of years. The most prolific of these is the fear and disempowerment that has been daily thrust in our faces causing humans to feel bad about themselves, both on a conscious and subconscious level, causing feelings of inadequacy, low self-esteem and low self-worth. These feelings are an energy that becomes embedded in cellular genetic memory. So not only are we affected by the current fear and disempowerment program of our current times, we are also affected by the genetic inheritance of past programming from our parents, their parents and way back through our ancestry.

It is my understanding that when we first inhabit a physical body at birth, this genetic memory is sitting dormant in cellular memory but becomes "activated" the very first time we experience fear or being put down as a small child. The aforementioned negative conditioning in cellular memory then surges up into our awareness first on a subconscious level, which can then filter into our conscious self, causing us to feel doubt, fear, low self-esteem and a low self-value. This then causes us another major problem as we are all actually powerful "creators" and we create our own reality moment by moment. It has been revealed to me by personal experience that the realities we create for ourselves will always be a "mirror" of the "view" we hold of ourselves both consciously and subconsciously which is where the "minefield" (mind-field) exists, for we have already established that the subconscious view of ourselves is tainted by cellular memory of the fear based programming from our ancestry. To give an example of how this might play itself out in our reality, the kind of person that is self-destructive in their view of themselves by being highly self-critical or mentally beating themselves up will literally manifest someone in their life that will play that role for them as a mirror. This is a sobering thought but in actuality a very powerful and empowering understanding. For to choose to adopt this simple understanding one would never feel like a "victim" of their reality, for they would view any situation of circumstance that comes into their life as a gift even though it might not be a pleasant experience, as it would bring their attention to some aspect or residue of old conditioning or programming that they haven't dealt with or harmonized. Then instead of looking at the external manifestation of this for an answer they need only look within themselves for the resolution and therefore would always be in their own personal power.

It has therefore also been my personal experience that some of our most powerful gifts have often come wrapped up in ugly packaging! It is for this reason that in my own workshops, talks and in my TV show, I put a great deal of emphasis on self-empowerment and self-nurturing, providing simple tools for people to bring this about. I encourage people to take time out for themselves when they need to without feeling guilty about it. I encourage people to do things that bring them joy and make them feel good about themselves. For me personally whenever I am faced with decisions or choices I will always choose the one that "makes my heart sing!"

The most powerful form of self-nurturing as far as I am concerned is spending frequent times out in Nature, by the lakes, rivers, forests and trees and by the ocean, allowing myself just to "be" immersed in that environment, breathing in the life force and being totally at "one" with the beauty and splendor that surrounds me. If I have issues that I need to deal with that may be causing me concern or stress I will immediately go to my favorite place in Nature and allow the energies to permeate my being until I feel a sense of peace and well-being. Only then will I work at the problem. Amazingly, my feelings are nourished by Nature and very often a change in attitude results in the issue at hand not seeming to be such a big deal after all!

Another big bonus for self-nurturing oneself is that not only will this change the view of oneself to a positive one and therefore our reality will mirror this and attract like a magnet positive opportunities and realities, but it also raises our own personal vibration which then raises the vibration on the planet – for we are all actually "one" with everything in existence. All we perceive as being external to us is contained within us. It is only an illusion that we are separate. The implications of this are immense. Not only are we "one" and a part of Nature, we are also "one" with the universe, multi-verses and all that we perceive as being "out there" in the great beyond. This to me is the underlying concept of the term "spirituality," and is what the Ancient Code is really all about.

Many people think that spirituality or being spiritual is related to religion. True spirituality is beyond religion, so in other words one doesn't have to be religious to be spiritual. Having said that, many of the religions of the world in their original format had intended spirituality to be the basis of their understanding. Unfortunately individuals with personal or political agendas have perverted many of their original teachings to suit their own ends and religion then became a means of controlling or separating the masses by instigating fear and disempowerment. From my own personal research and understanding the fear and disempowerment program has been running on this planet for thousands of years and of course still does to this day! No wonder so many people have issues with themselves suffering from low self-worth or self-esteem or feel totally disempowered. Their reality then mirrors this negative tainted view of themselves and just further perpetuates further disempowered manifestations in their life. Hence the reason I put such an emphasis on self-nurturing, which includes self-love, honoring, valuing and being "true" to oneself, and being in your own integrity. To me, I would have to say that the change we make ourselves to simply love and honor ourselves would be one of the most, if not the most, powerful forces of change and betterment for the planet.

When I was younger many individuals including myself would feel an impulse to discover the "truth" of things. As previously mentioned I have always had an ability or perhaps a "gift" that no matter how complex or complicated a concept or idea may be, I am able to break it down to its simplest level of understanding. So when I wish to know whether something is truth or not, it seems logical to me that as long as I live my life being as truthful as I can be in all my endeavors, relationships with other people and of course especially to myself, I am in the "vibration" of truth. Therefore when presented with any concept or idea I will either resonate with it or not. Another way of putting this idea across would be observing those things that "feel right" to us, or not. This simple concept of understanding has served me very well on my own personal journey and has revealed many extraordinary insights and powerful manifestation tools.

The idea and concept that "we are all one" that many ancient esoteric spiritual teachings have conveyed for eons is now being discovered in recent scientific research too, specifically from the realm of Quantum Physics. Quantum Physicists refer to the concept of the "Holographic Universe" wherein everything is contained within everything else in existence, even the most minuscule particle contains the whole. Separation is just an illusion. These scientists may use different terminology from our ancient ancestor's teachings, but they are saying the same thing!

This is extremely exciting and inspiring to me that we are seeing science and spirituality start to unite. This can only bring about a greater awareness to the many individuals that insist on scientific "proof" before they entertain anything that may be unfamiliar to them, particular when relating to those things that are regarded as the paranormal which includes psychic abilities, ESP (Extra Sensory Perception), unconventional healing practices and communication with the "spirit" world. Quantum Science has discovered that there are other dimensions of reality all co-existing in the same space but on different vibrational frequencies, and they refer to this as the multi-dimensional universe. Spiritualists refer to this as multiple spiritual planes. The Bible even refers to "God's house of many mansions."

It is totally acceptable to me and from my own personal experience that consciousness is contained within all that exists, so the idea of communicating with another consciousness that exists in another dimension – either as beings in form or as just energies – is entirely feasible to me. I have had overwhelming evidence and proof of this in my own personal reality working as a Psychic Artist whereby I channel and draw many beings known as "Spirit Guides." These can include beings that are referred to as Angels, Elfin/Faery Kingdom (also know as Elementals or Nature Spirits), Ancient Ancestors and even beings from other Star Systems that I refer to as "Star Beings."

All we need is an open heart and open mind to entertain that which is considered beyond the "norm," and free ourselves from rigid dogma or conditioning, to explore new and untold possibilities. Time and time again we have seen in our own lifetimes that things that were once thought impossible have now become possible and are even a part of our normal everyday reality. Laser beams, microchips, space shuttles and genetic engineering to name but a few. In my reality anything is possible and anything we can imagine could one day be possible.

I would like to leave you with this thought…

If you were to accept the evidence and proof that "we are all one" knowing that everything you think and do affects the whole of existence, what would you do?

Many people have said to me that they wish there was more love, caring, honor, respect and peace in the world. My answer to them is that if they were to choose to become all these things by holding these qualities within themselves, they will have created more of that in their world and it will be so. We are the creators of our own reality. Dream, imagine and visualize your most magnificent of realities and then become it!

Fundamentally we have two choices in these current times; to either act from fear, or to act from LOVE. I know what I choose.

#

Nick Ashron is a Psychic Artist, Musician and Author who has gained much recognition in the spiritual arena over the past 30 years having been featured in holistic publications, TV shows, spiritual films & DVDs (including *Ancient Code - The Movie*), and having been a regular exhibitor at Mind Body Spirit Events throughout the UK and in the USA. Nick runs Workshops on

Self-Empowerment and was voted "Popular Spiritual/Psychic Artist" in the Spiritual ConneXtions Acknowledgment Awards in 2008.

Nick also hosts his own TV show called *Nick Ashron's Lightworker's Guide to the Galaxy*, which is an alternative chat show expanding awareness of the vast arena of spirituality, and seeks to support individuals on their journey towards self awareness, spiritual expansion, peace and fulfillment.

For more information on all of Nick's work visit www.nickashron.com.

The False Dilemma
Ancient Inroads Towards a New Age

By Philip Coppens

According to Hindu tradition, an era known as Kali Yuga began in either January or February of 3102 BC. For some, it is said to last 432,000 years, while others claim it has already ended, or is about to end. Either way, all accept that the Kali Yuga is a gradual forgetting of our divine origins, a fall into matter, or a "solidification," to quote the term used by the French alternative philosopher René Guénon. Coincidentally, 3100 BC roughly marks the beginning of the ancient Egyptian civilization, as well as the beginning of the Mayan Calendar, which is to end in 2012 AD. In short, it seems that "civilization" coincides with the Kali Yuga and both are definitely defined by materialism.

Equally, the 8th century BC Greek poet Hesiod, spoke of a Golden Age, Silver Age, Bronze Age and finally, the current age, that of iron. Iron definitely defines our era: our primary modes of transport (car, ship, plane and train) are all metallic; many of our modern buildings and most of our bridges rely on it; our modern household appliances (fridges, cookers, washing machines) have it as one of their main components. Still, it is said that our ancient ancestors were afraid of iron, for it was believed that it did something to the soul. Specifically, it was said to deny or inhibit access to spiritual realms. It is said that civilizations who knew of iron, refused to use it in the construction of their monuments to the dead. If so, since, it is clear that we have come to embrace iron. Indeed, we might assume that the Iron Age is something of prehistory, but in truth, it defines our modern era even better.

Whether we look at the labyrinth of Knossos on the Greek island of Crete, or the Turkish Çatal Hüyük, or the hypogea on the Italian island of Sardinia, we find the depictions of the bull. Interestingly, Hinduism links morality with a bull, known as Dharma. The tradition explains that in the first age, the Satya Yuga, the bull had four legs; in each successive age, morality declined, each age taking one leg of the animal: the bull today therefore has only one leg. No wonder therefore that our time is seen as a Dark Age, when Mankind is the furthest possible from God. It is linked with the demon Kali, who stands for strife, discord, quarrel and contention, which is an apt description of a century in which tens of millions of people died in two world wars.

Robert Schwartz in *Courageous Souls* relates that, "during the course of my research, I came across a young man who in meditation contacted a future self, that is, an incarnation of his soul at a future time. The future self told him that people of the future refer to this time on Earth as 'The Fear Ages.'" Schwartz observes that fear is the predominant emotion of our time, part of our daily existence to such an extent that we no longer tend to notice it: television and newspaper news is one continuous stream of scare mongering, aided by governments that underline the don'ts and dangers.

Contrast this with the ancient Egyptian frame of mind, which was that of Maat: the world consisted of two forces, order and chaos, whereby it was the task of the ruler to balance these.

Fear is a repressive force, which stifles creativity, which is precisely why the Western economy in the past twenty years has gone through a series of artificial "happy pills": the dot.com bubble – which burst – the housing market – which collapsed – and the introduction of surveillance systems anywhere is not so much the implementation of a Big Brother agenda, but a desperate attempt to inject novelty into a dying economy, one that was based on greed, an altogether not very noble principle; in fact, one of the seven cardinal sins.

The desperation of the old paradigm is made apparent when the solution to the 2008-9 collapse of the finance industry was seen as a mixture of fiscal stimulus, greater regulation and new structures, in short, Big Brother methodologies and more of the same. Economic experts, however, noted that what was truly needed was a call for moral behavior, as it was the lack of, which created the demise of the old economic paradigm. For centuries, usury was banned by the Church. Debt in Judaism is seen as a form of slavery. Sharia banking still forbids usury. The "Christian West," however, had served the daemon Mammon. But, as if the goddess Maat will indeed always see balance once the scale has tipped too far in one direction, the financial crisis itself burnt off the labors of greed.

Still, greed projected on the masses equals comfort. And whereas the collapse of the financial markets burnt off the sin of greed, Man's dependency on comfort remains more than ever intact.

Amidst the viral infection that was monetary greed, the world has also seen a tremendous amount of novelty. In 1995, I was one of the first to have non-office email access. In 1999, at least in Britain, free email accounts were offered. Broadband only came into full swing a few years later. Since, we have digital TV, digital cameras, and now digital camcorders. Today, we have integrated mobile technology into our daily lives, but as with any new phenomenon, we have not yet matured to it completely: we use it at inconvenient moments, while a survey showed that some Blackberrys remain close to the bed, so that the noise of an incoming message will awaken the person, and he or she can reply to it.

But in less than one decade, the world has become a radically different place and it has become a Crystal Age, or sand, the basic ingredients upon which we store all the information we call computer technology. Equally, with a revolution in the airline and car industry, for the first time, the world truly is a global village. For the first time in history, we are contacted to almost anywhere on the globe, and can be anywhere on the globe, at affordable prices, in less than two days.

Still, this New World is only there as a capability, which relatively few use. Fact of the matter is that though we can get halfway across the world in a day, this at a price of less than your average month's wages, it is equally a fact that we fear the world "out there" and cannot – we think – safely visit large portions of our world; many Europeans are afraid of visiting, let alone renting cars, in the States and we all "know" that most of the Middle East, including Egypt, is a den of terrorism and haters of the West. Alas, only a few decades ago, we conquered the final frontier, space, but today, many are scared to walk through a neighborhood park at night.

Where is spirituality in all of this? In the Kali Yuga, spirituality has degenerated into religion, and religion has descended into fundamentalism. We live in a time where the Catholic faith has condemned *The Da Vinci Code*, and Islam *The Satanic Verses*. Both are novels. It was once said that faith could move mountains, and faith was at the heart of the Crusades. But today, it seems, faith is fragile, dogmatic, and shaken by – mediocre – novels. Religious institutions have become afraid, and feel they have to defend their dogma, rather than "go with the flow" and adapt where needed and should see this as a sign of strength and versatility. When fear rages through the corridors of both state and church, we are indeed in an Age of Fear.

Kathleen McGowan in her book *The Book of Love* highlights how the re-emerging face of Christianity as defined by the discovery of the *Nag Hammadi* gospels and the *Dead Sea Scrolls,* which formed the inspiration for *The Da Vinci Code,* reveals an altogether gentler, more loving side to Jesus. It is a face of Christianity that dogma and political power removed from that religion in the third century AD. When in the 20th century, the *Nag Hammadi* and *Dead Sea Scrolls* were recovered, the Church showed its worst face, trying to control the translation and thus hoping that if anything were to be uncovered that would go against the Church doctrine, power could stifle that which might reveal a truth. It is no doubt ironic that whereas the Church was able to do just that, shortly afterwards, it was unable to do anything about the interest created by *The Da Vinci Code* and like. McGowan, however, queries why simple teachings of love and faith and community would be considered more dangerous today than they ever were, and why the Church so desperately tries to suppress this message of love. It is, perhaps nothing more or less, an expression of our "zeitgeist," the spirit of our time.

What has happened to us? Whatever fear one tackles, at the core, is the realization that what we fear, is the unknown. We fear "them" and this fear is for some expressed as a conspiracy theory of how "they" are out "there" to get "us." For some, "them" are terrorists, an evil conspiracy of Illuminati, or a neighbor or family member who has it "in" for "us." Our age is one of "us" versus "them" – and "they" are never truly identified, which is why there is such fear. It is the chaos of "them" "out there" that is believed to upset our natural order. But where is the balance, Maat? Worse: where is the sense of community, required to maintain that balance?

When we look at monuments like the Great Pyramids, or Stonehenge, we now know that these were not built by evil rulers using slave labor. Instead, we know that the pyramids were built by ordinary people, who were well looked after, and who achieved a seemingly impossible task, because they were doing it for the greater good: it was a community project and the result is, in the case of the Great Pyramid, the only surviving wonder of the world, a structure that has stood there for at least 4000 years, and – unless we decide to tear it down – will stand there eternally. What structures of modern society will survive? What truly common building projects have we achieved in recent decades? When you look at Britain, the country chosen to deliver the 2012 Olympics and hence the nation that should best reflect the mood of our times, you find great internal division over the Olympic Games – a last vestige of collaboration, though more and more eroded in controversy and strife.

Instead, the largest buildings Mankind has recently built are normally financial towers, monuments of greed, like the Twin Towers of New York. They symbolized greed and avarice so much, that their destruction became a symbol of destroying the Western hegemony. It is therefore clear that for the 20th century, greed was the new religion. 9/11, whether a true terrorist event or the result of some form of conspiracy, underlines the us versus them mentality, the central feature of the Fear Ages.

What do we truly fear? Comfort is the key determinative of our time. It is what drives our economy, what is responsible for clinical obesity in large sections of the Western world, and it is the one thing we fear losing – and hence why we live in the Fear Ages.

It is little reported that the dawn of civilization, linked with a sedentary lifestyle and hence the need for agriculture, is vastly different from what most assume.

Anthropological and archaeological studies have shown that the sedentary lifestyle was undesired by many of our roaming hunter-gatherer ancestors. Agriculture required a discipline, resulted into economics (the exchange of goods), based on more measured values, with money being the sum of it all. Money was a means to measure, but in the end, it became – and is – the end, though it is clear that its end, to some extent, is now occurring: money is once again being introduced within a real framework, where it always should have sat, but from which it began to escape from the 12th century onwards … interestingly, in a mechanism that was developed by those infamous Knights Templar. They devised the idea that any pilgrim or, specifically, crusader, could deposit money e.g. in France upon his departure, and, once in the Middle East or back in France after the voyage, could have access to it; the check was born. Of course, many of these people died en-route, which explains the wealth of the Knights Templar. And their demise on Friday, October 13, 1307 on specific orders of the French king has always been seen as something extremely negative, but, at the same time, it is equally a fact that the king did precisely what he had to do to keep the virus of greed from destroying his nation. 700 years later, all Western nations were required to "bail out" the banks – history had repeated itself, but this time, the financial greed had become so widespread, that a system that should have been obliterated, had to be kept artificially ticking over.

So how do we rectify our problems? What we have forgotten, is the creative imagination, a sense of exploration. We rarely "boldly go," and we might argue it is because wherever we go, someone has gone before. But there is a difference between a voyage as Mankind, and a voyage of Man. Mankind is making giant leaps all the time, but we have forgotten how to make small steps for individual men, embedded as we have become within the repetitive habit of comfort; we no longer leave – in all senses of the world – our "comfort zone."

This is supported by a media who builds up heroes in days and is then quick to pull these people down – showing how very human they are. And, indeed, why would anyone want to excel, when it appears that "they" are out "there" to pull "us" down? Equally, our modern heroes have been defined by overcoming a particular weakness: Richard Branson has dyslexia and Stephen Hawking can no longer speak, but there is no global figure of global transformation, though Nelson Mandela is perhaps the closest modern hero we have, after Gandhi's death. No one else comes close. Where are the heroes of the old Homeric hymns?

Was it any different in the past? It might not appear to be, as we currently see history as a continuous sequence of wars and strife. By focusing on wars, the chaos, we have redefined history as a series of fears. In truth, history is nothing of the kind. We remember the pyramids and temples of Egypt; we remember the paintings of the Renaissance; the relics of the past, that which has survived, and what sits inside our museums. These are examples of exploration, if only because of the tales faced by explorers. Take the Mitchell-Hedges crystal skull. A genuine mysterious artifact, brought to Britain by a larger than life character, who uttered the words: "Life which is lived without zest and adventure is not life at all."

Rather than trying to explore this artifact and the cultures to which it belonged, all discussions focus either on absurd new age stories, or bullying tactics by the powers that be and who claim to know it all, and who claim that no genuine mystery is present there, or anywhere else. Science does not explore death; it treats near death experiences with disdain; ghosts and the like are fodder for sensationalist television programs and scorn of newspaper editors. We know it all, and there is nothing to explore. Move along, nothing to see, nothing remaining to be explored. The biggest falsehood of our times have been achieved by, once again, reducing the big world out there, just like the city lights have blocked out the big expanse of the night's sky. We can literally only see as high as the tallest skyscraper and the next block, even though we negotiate towns in cars that could keep going from sea to sea, country to country, if we wanted to. Instead, a drive to get the morning paper, the supermarket and shopping mall are our modern explorations. For all the rest, we need television, in all of its reductionism of what reality is: reality television, which is scripted from the first to the last minute – fooling the audience even more. Fear has meant that we have tools of exploration at our disposal, which we never use. We have 4x4's but how many have ever been off-road, let alone on a gravel path?

The proof, as always, is in art. Art is an expression of the artist's inner world, an introversion/introvision, made – created – in this world: the extravert phase, which brings the balance, the realization. But today's art lacks the inner vision, highlighted by the leading artists of our time, whereby an unmade bed going for millions (Tracy Emin) is seen as art. It is, as it typifies our era. And Emin is therefore – alas – a true artist.

There might nevertheless be good news. As mentioned, the age of Iron is turning to crystal and sand and though many are seeing the negative – we do, after all, live in the Fear Ages – of the new technology, the fact of the matter is that it has the potential to liberate us.

For one, our window on the world, is a monitor, whether computer or television and we spend endless time in front of it. Television is becoming more interactive and with digital television, we become master of seeing what we want to see, when. The "slave phase" of that medium is nearly over. Though many see mobile technology as a dependency, the fact is that mobile technology is the right type of technology: it is mobile. The fixed landline meant we could only communicate whenever we were physically near a device; today we can phone when desired. Though at present we use it quite often too often for no real purpose, this comes with everything novel, and will wear off over time.

Technology will be able – and is beginning to – work directly on the brain, providing vision of different realities which previously only hallucinogenics were able to offer us. Politically, our attitude towards drugs remains warped. Following 9/11, the West invaded Afghanistan while that country's primary source of income – the opium poppy – had been almost eradicated by the Taliban regime. During the first year of Western occupation, Afghanistan instead reported a record-breaking harvest of opium.

Remarkably, developments in computer technology are not linear. The computer had created virtual worlds long before we realized the computer could be used for "social networking:" the very type of community and sharing that was – and to a large extent remains – missing in society, but which was key to our ancestors.

But look at the computer communication methodology of a decade ago – chat rooms and especially forums – and look at MySpace and Facebook, and you will see an enormously different "feel factor." Chat rooms were populated by people who logged on under aliases and acted out inner fantasies with which reality could not cope. Forums were – and largely remain – a platform for ego trips and quarrels. The name "forum" was therefore aptly named, as in the olden days, it was where the village gathered to gossip and "popularly condemn" certain members of society. In fact, at one stage, I joked that World War III was likely to start on a forum.

The newer social networking sites are far more ... social. We have friends and we can drop them if we have experienced any negativity from them. About one year ago, I had a dozen or so friends on Facebook. Since, that number has risen to more than 300. A year ago, I made contact with a friend of a friend in Malta and spent a most enjoyable day with her. As a result, this technology had given me the opportunity to meet a new friend, purely through the power of Facebook. Since, I have become reacquainted with school friends and others whom I hadn't seen for years, purely because the means of staying in touch were not adequate enough for both our personal circumstances. I have met other "Facebook friends" since at conferences and lectures and through their "status," I know what concerns them and whether it all goes swimmingly, or whether some need a more "human touch." I can be in "touch" with them easily, and almost instantaneously. A weekly telephone conversation with my parents has reduced in length, to deeper and more essential conversations, as all the "what did you do in the past week" has been cut down: my mother has read it already, and knows my state of mind, via Facebook.

In medieval times, maps placed dragons and other creatures at the edge of the explored world: beyond, danger lied. Brave sailors nevertheless set course for new worlds, even though they apparently believed the world was not round, and they therefore might just fall into an unknown abyss. In the 20th century, brave men crawled into the dark confined quarters of space capsules to explore a world beyond this Earth. Some, like Edgar Mitchell, had mystical experiences, making him no doubt the first human, extra-terrestrial shaman. His message, unfortunately, has become lost and NASA, which once symbolized the boldly going to where no man had gone before, has become the topic of intrigue, with accusations that we never went to the moon and that they are hiding many things.

Our times will indeed be marked as the Ages of Fear. Though Columbus will have known fear, he faced it, and boldly went. We fear the world will end, whether through a nuclear holocaust or manmade global warming – the latest in a series of "fear campaigns" that tells us that we now need to fear not just the Red Menace outside, nor the terrorist living within our society, but we need to fear ourselves. We cannot be trusted, not with cigarettes, alcohol, food, sex, and soon, no doubt, the amount of times per minute we breathe. Those who believe they are free, have instead fallen for extra-terrestrial fears, with claims that "they" will imminently arrive, either to free or to enslave it, or alternatively the magic – or doom – of 2012 and the end of the Mayan calendar, the prophecies of Nostradamus, etc., while the "anti-establishment" tells us we need to fear that establishment, which is here to control us, enslave us – sometimes, apparently, in cahoots with these evil aliens. Those whom many believe have liberated themselves from the false belief of religion, have merely fallen for a new threat, and have accentuated that fear, and normally also believe that resistance is futile, as "they" are Big Brother and all powerful. After all, "they" covered up the existence of alien life, have UFOs in storage in secret government facilities, and … not even all presidents are told of this.

Fear has a paralyzing effect. In truth, "they" who control – the elected officials – are as afraid as we are, and most often afraid of us, and how we will react and whether their decisions will be popular or not. Therefore, when a country like the United States is facing a new fear – an economic downturn – the elected officials instead will focus on the question whether or not non-human primates – monkeys – should be allowed to cross federal borders. Faced with something we cannot address, we look elsewhere and build up nothing into something. It is equally what has happened with our modern heroes, who come from nowhere, and largely have never gone anywhere. They are not, alas, true heroes and even the last great heroes – the astronauts – are, as just mentioned, now quite often seen as fake: that the moon landings were all hoaxed and staged. Fear and ridicule go hand in hand, for the mind thinks that if we ridicule something, it becomes less fearful.

We human primates have become ostriches. The ostrich is said to bury his head in the sand when it is fearful, for that way, it will at least not see what happens next. Since many years, we live in an age of ostrich politics. Whether we accept it or not, fear has paralyzed us, at this moment in time from the waist down, but potentially soon, from the neck down. Like a paralyzed person, Mankind needs help with so many things, and feels like no-one is able to provide it. We look to God Out There, ET, or whomever, without realizing that it is not they who have paralyzed us in a beam of light emanating from His finger or their spaceship, but that our fear is entirely homebrewed, manmade … and imaginary.

The imaginary is today the bailiwick of the computer. The computer is slowly integrating with our physical self. A bionic eye will allow us to interface directly with a virtual world. At the moment, virtual worlds largely are reflections of our "reality:" we buy and sell virtual real estate in Second Life and do all the mundane and materialistic tasks there. The old adage of "As Above, So Below," has become "As here, so on the computer." So far, it seems, no one has realized that this virtual world can be as hallucinogenic as we want it to be. The sky and the power of our imagination are the limit. In short, the virtual world of the computer can become true art: the programmer who today programs boring lines of code, can transform that code into a liberating framework, a virtual construct, which can become the art of the 21st century. It will be sacred space, for what we are able to do there, could be on par with the visionary experiences of the shaman. All it needs is a shamanically-inspired programmer, and a new world will be created. Everyone in the world would

– could – be introduced to the power of the mind, free from the body. Technology can deliver, and could deliver, within a matter of years. It is as easy, and as close, as that. The only "problem" is that someone needs to "just do it."

In the 17th century, science "as such" became defined: it broke from the ranks of religion, and in the West went its separate ways. Many will argue that since, it has lost its morality, also fell for the daemon of greed, but also because science is now able to venture anywhere – from abortion, cloning to genetic modification of various forms of life – without a clear plan as to why precisely some of these scientific revolutions occur. Indeed, however great the cloning of a sheep may be from a scientific point of view, what is the point, precisely?

At the same time, the science of archaeology is slowly beginning to uncover radically different origins of Mankind; the world of geology and archaeology has broken the idea that the world was created in 4004 BC. We are beginning to unveil older beginnings, and can only wonder in awe at the cave paintings in northern Spain and Southern France, painted by our ancestors more than 20,000 years ago. In the 20th century, culminating in the 1990s, alternative theories of archaeology focused on a lost Golden Age: Atlantis, Lemuria, the Sphinx. In the 21st century, these belief systems are both confirmed and abandoned: archaeology has uncovered evidence of extremely ancient cultural sites, like Göbekli Tepe, 12,000 years old. That Golden Age is not "lost;" we are uncovering it, and we can learn its lessons, if we so desire.

But archaeology itself, its publication, popularization and integration within society is a slow process. The matter is complicated as science is not interested in the mind. Egyptian religion for example, apart from surveying which deity was what, is totally left untouched by academics. Science cares greatly about seeing the body as a machine that can be operated, changed, improved, but it has no interest in looking at the mind, its processing unit. Indeed, the shaman was a scientist of the mind, exploring it both inside and outside of the body, but modern science shies away from studying hallucinogenic or (near) death experiences, and largely doesn't even touch the mind within the body. As a whole, science has therefore removed the spirit from everyday existence, arguing – on what basis? – that it is a matter of religion, or psychology – a "soft science." But it is a matter of fact that our brain is hardware. And would you tell a computer programmer that whereas the machine he is working on is hard science, the lines of code he has written, is soft science and that he is therefore inferior to the hardware specialists? The fact of the matter is that a computer without software, is useless. Absolutely worthless. Yet we somehow believe that is not the case for the human body and the mind? And we do not hold scientists accountable for this lack of ambition, this unwillingness to take a step into the unknown and explore? But wasn't that what science was apparently all about, and why it broke away from the bonds of religion, as it was apparently only meant to confirm the existing dogma?

In the Dark Ages of the Mind, in which we are now in, there is great polarization. We see the world as bad versus evil, the "material world," which quantum physics tells us is nevertheless not at all that "material" and which actually relies on the disposition of thought – the mind – to decide what's what. Indeed, quantum physics has put the mind back into the centre of reality and is telling – painfully slowly and quietly, it has to be said – Mankind that this "real world" is as fictitious as the virtual computer worlds we have created. It is a world held together by a type of "consensus" of all of us: we live in a consensus reality.

I find it greatly amusing that in the 1970s, Uri Geller bent a metal – iron – spoon as a sign of defiance to this paradigm. When the experiments were broadcast, hundreds of children in front of televisions all of a sudden began to bend spoons too. Their parents had not yet told them that we apparently couldn't bend metal, as metal just doesn't do that kind of thing. But for a mind not yet told it cannot, it clearly could.

One of the enlightened thinkers of the 20th century was Carl Gustav Jung. He studied under Sigmund Freud, who believed – despite while in London living just a few blocks from the residence of theosophist Helena Blavatsky – that everything about the mind was reductionist, and often the result of… fear or negative experiences. Jung, instead, was an explorer of the mind and had mystical experiences of his own. At the end of his life, he even focused on UFOs and linked them, and various other aspects he observed within the Western world of the 1950s, as an embryo of the "Age of Aquarius:" a new era. Or, perhaps, the end of the Kali Yuga.

Fact of the matter is that we are close. All the building blocks are there, though in truth, have always been there. The problem is that we remain polarized. One of the great "illnesses" of our times is "bipolarisation" and the fact of the matter is that Mankind as a whole is bipolar. It is either black or white, but in truth, the world is all grey. The debate is not whether God exists or not, which is a debate used so as to avoid talking about morality and the greater common good, which is the Go(o)d we should embrace and strive for, whether or not there is a larger power out there. The fact of the matter is, that this greater Good is good for all of us, and each of us. We simply need to realize that there is middle ground and that it is this middle ground, the area of consensus, socialism and community, which is what needs to be sought. The last century has taught us that communism didn't work, but it is clearly that capitalism as such doesn't work either. It's a realization that is slowly dawning.

There is a need for middle ground: the excluded middle which in our Age of Fear and materialism, has always been lacking. We burnt witches and we condemn those with a different view of our world. As to those who have a different view of reality, they do not even get discussed, or convene in forgotten villages or towns and live in "communities", which should be seen not as an example of communism, but of social interaction, which not necessarily serve as a model for the New Age, but is nevertheless evidence that it can work, and from which we can learn the positives. And there is evidence that this is working. After Europe experienced two world wars that divided it not only during the wars, but for four decades after the second as well, Europe is now beginning to work collectively, as a union. And it will be up to leaders of nations to lead, rather than find excuses.

The problem is that we – typical of the Kali Yuga – still operate within the fallacy of a false dilemma, (the either-or fallacy), in which we believe that any situation has only two alternatives, black or white, and only those are considered, when in fact there are other options. In fact, the best outcome is often a synthesis, of the old and the new: the ancient code that remains present and accessible to us, and which science has and is uncovering, but which needs to be fed back into our present civilization, to enrich it, and to steer it upwards again. It is the path of the excluded middle, or the excluded third. At some point in time, the Latin phrase "Tertium non datur" was coined: "there is no third (possibility)." There is a third possibility. That is the Ancient Code.

#

Philip Coppens (1971-) started his career as an investigative journalist, with specialist subject the world of politics and intelligence agencies. As a result, material uncovered on the life of President John F. Kennedy's alleged assassin, Lee Harvey Oswald, was used by a US government enquiry in 1994.

In 1995, he established *Frontier Magazine* (formerly Frontier 2000) together with *Herman Hegge,* a newsstand magazine in the Netherlands and Belgium, creating a series of scoops such as confirmation of the existence of pyramids in China. These and other often groundbreaking articles have resulted in a series of articles appearing in various magazines (*Fortean Times, NEXUS, Hera, Fenix, Mysterien, New Dawn, Atlantis Rising, Ancient American, Paranoia Magazine,* etc.), as well as appearances on television (Belgium's *Kanaal 2* and *VRT* news, *Voyager* (RaiDue - Italy), *Edge Media TV*, etc.) and radio (*Swiss International Radio, Dreamland Radio, The X-Zone* (Talkstar Radio), *Eye on the Future, RedIce Creations, Eerie Radio*, etc.). Since 1995, Frontier Sciences Foundation has grown to incorporate, amongst others, Frontier Bookshop and Frontier Publishing.

In 1999, he was the principal researcher for Lynn Picknett and Clive Prince's *The Stargate Conspiracy,* which investigated current politician's apparent obsession with ancient Egypt.

The Code of the Copper Scroll

By Robert Feather, MIMMM, C. Eng.

Within the collection of Dead Sea Scrolls, found in caves near Khirbet Qumran, one stands out as being unique in its content and the material on which it was written. Engraved on very pure copper, it was discovered by Henri de Contenson in 1952 in a cave, now known as Cave 3, on the western shores of the Dead Sea.

The tightly rolled scroll, heavily oxidized and broken into two pieces, defied attempts to open it until it was taken to Manchester College of Science and Technology in 1955-56 and cut open under the guidance of John Allegro. Allegro was part of the official team working on the Scrolls at the École Biblique in East Jerusalem and he was the first person to produce a translation of the ancient Hebrew writing and publish his findings in *The Treasure of the Copper Scroll*.[1]

John Allegro examining part of the opened Copper Scroll in Manchester.

The Copper Scroll originally comprised three sheets of 99.8% pure copper riveted together to form a 2.4m long, by 0.3m wide, 1mm thick scroll on which was engraved a list of some 64 locations where priceless amounts of treasure and ritual material were buried. Allegro soon mounted an expedition to Israel to search for the treasures, but despite numerous attempts by him and scores of other treasure seekers no one found any of the hidden items --- until I started investigating the problem in the late 1990s!

Whilst most of the text was written in a Herodian style, 1st century BCE Hebrew, interspersed among the columns were 13 Greek letters, which baffled scholars and were considered yet another puzzle of what was already one of the most enigmatic of the Dead Sea Scrolls. Explanations ranged from the letters being coded abbreviations for treasure locations, names of the people who hid them, descriptions of the treasures, and instructions for their recovery etc. [2] None of these suggestions is anything other than guesswork and there is no agreement amongst scholars about their meaning.

A translation of Column 1 of the Copper Scroll text is typical of the style and content:

> *the ruin which is in the valley, pass under*
> *the steps leading to the East*
> *40 cubits (...) a chest of money and its total*
> *the weight of 17 talents.* ΚεΝ
> *In the sepulchral monument, in the third course:*
> *one hundred gold ingots. In the great cistern of the courtyard*
> *of the peri-style, in a hollow in the floor covered with sediment,*
> *in front of the upper opening: nine hundred talents.*
> *In the hill of Kochlit, tithe-vessels of the lord of the peoples and sacred*
> *vestments; total of the tithes and of the treasure; a seventh of the*
> *second tithe made unclean. Its opening lies on the edges of the Northern*
> *channel, six cubits in the direction of the cave of the ablutions,* ΧΑΓ
> *In the plastered cistern Manos, going down to the left,*
> *at a height of three cubits from the bottom: silver, forty*
> *...talents...*

When I started studying the Copper Scroll, around 1996, initially from a metallurgical point of view, I concluded that the form of engraving and material of use was unknown for the period and more associated with work being produced in Egypt from a thousand years earlier. There were also clear examples of Egyptian hieratic numbers in the terms assigned to the weights of the treasures being listed. This perspective led me to look at the mysterious Greek letters from an Egyptian standpoint and make a startling discovery. When the first 10 Greek letters are placed together from four different sections of the Scroll they spell out the name of an Egyptian Pharaoh by the name of Akhenaten!

The letters are interspersed in the columns as:

K ε N # X A Γ # H N # Θ ε # Δ I # T P # Σ K

* The Greek letters X Γ and Θ have English transliterations of kh, g and th, respectively.

Initially many Dead Sea Scrolls academics were skeptical about my interpretation, despite the fact that most of them knew little about the Egyptian language or the pharaohnic period, and almost none of them had ever been to Amarna, the site of Pharaoh Akhenaten's Holy City. Other scholars have since come round to accepting my reading and two of the foremost Egyptian/Greek language scholars, Professor John Tait, of University College, London, and Professor Rosalie David, of Manchester University agreed that my reading of the Pharaoh's name was quite plausible, especially as his name had been expunged from Egyptian literature, and the Greek letters appearing in the Copper Scroll some 1300 years after his death might well be the most appropriate to enunciate his name.

The significance of the finding of this long forgotten Pharaoh's name in a Jewish document of the 1st century BCE is profound. Not only did it enable me to locate some of the treasure items listed in the Copper Scroll, it helps validate a connection for the Hebrews all the way back to Egypt in pre-Exodus times – a connection that is fully detailed in some of my books. [3]

Perhaps the most important element of this connection is the example and message of a lifestyle and beliefs that this enlightened Pharaoh sends down through the ages to us in our present world of strife and conflicts. Pharaoh Akhenaten was far ahead of his time and his view of humanity, existential belief, the desired relationship between people, and morality has a lot to tell us, even now. He postulated a supreme force for good as being behind nature, existence and our wellbeing. He advocated and practiced complete equality between sexes and social classes, in religion and society. Much of his philosophy was set out in his Great Hymn, which can still be seen chiseled in hieroglyphics on the tomb walls of one of his courtiers at El-Amarna, in central Egypt.

References

1. John Marco Allegro, *The Treasure of the Copper Scroll*, Routledge & Kegan Paul, 1961.
2. Al Wolters, *The Copper Scroll – Overview, Text and Translation*, Sheffield Academic Press, 1996.
3. Robert Feather, *The Mystery of the Copper Scroll of Qumran*, Inner Traditions, 2003.
4. Robert Feather, *The Secret Initiation of Jesus at Qumran*, Watkins/Baird, 2006.

© R. Feather 2009

# # #

Robert Feather was born in England and studied at Marylebone Grammar School and Sir John Cass College, London University, subsequently becoming a Member of the Institution of Metallurgists and a Chartered Engineer. Working initially in research for BICC, on precious metals casting, and the British Iron & Steel Federation he subsequently joined *Steel Times* as assistant editor and has spent some 25 years working in journalism and technical publishing. He has written for a wide cross-section of technical magazines, and was founder/editor of *The Metallurgist* and *Materials Technologist, official Journal of The Institution of Metallurgists*; editor of *Weighing & Measuring*, which dealt with metrology and the science of measuring; managing director of Uplands Press Ltd. and Lincoln Publications; director of Chess & Bridge Ltd. Throughout this time he has balanced his scientific career with a keen interest in history and social evolution, studying comparative religions and archaeology. He is a member of The Orion Center for the Study of the Dead Sea Scrolls and Associated Literature, The Egypt Exploration Society, and The Historical Metallurgy Society. His background and training as a Metallurgist and Chartered Engineer has given him a unique insight into the intricacies of The Copper Scroll, one of the most enigmatic of the Dead Sea Scrolls. This has resulted in him being retained as a consultant on a number of projects related to ancient metallic objects.

His first book has been translated into Dutch, Italian, Japanese and Portuguese, and was the subject of a BBC TV documentary, entitled *The Pharaoh's Holy Treasure*. Other TV documentaries include *The Spear of Jesus; Ramses: Wrath of God or Man;* and *The Copper Scroll - Digging for the Truth*.

The Forest

By Philip Gardiner

There was a forest, black as midnight and thicker than thieves. It was a favorite route for many, but suffered from highwaymen and robbers and so it was that four travelers found themselves needing to rest for the night, but fearful for their lives and possessions. They were good friends and three of them had been so for many years and so after discussion they decided to take turns to watch around the campfire. They settled down and the first watch went to a carpenter and wood sculptor. He sat for a while and then noticed a small length of wood and so decided to pass the time carving a beautiful image of a woman. By the time he had finished it was time for the next watch and so he placed the wooden lady down and woke his friend.

His friend was a tailor and after a while he too noticed the piece of wood and decided to make some clothes for the image of the woman. He produced a dress of silk and finished off with small leather sandals. Now it was time for him to sleep and he woke the next man who was a jeweler. Again to pass the time the jeweler decided to adorn the little figure with beautiful jewels. The final watch was summoned, but this time the man, a new friend the others had met on the journey, had no skills at all and so felt very ashamed of himself. He saw the wooden lady and admired the art and craft of his new friends. He wanted to show that he too was capable of improving upon the wood. He decided the only thing he could do was to seek the help of God and so he prayed:

"Oh, Almighty and Merciful Lord, give us some portion of your glory and as the Giver of Life bestow upon this humble figure the gift of life."

The fire finally went out and all was dark, all was one black place. Then the sun rose and crept across the landscape, revealing the countless forms that had been part of the darkness. One of these forms was now new to human life – the wooden woman was a living, breathing creature. The four men now awake were aghast and in awe at their creation. The wood carver admired the contours; the tailor was gushing with pride at the serene silken dress and the jeweler thought the fine gems were full of inspiration. And yet the fourth man claimed the upper hand for himself, because it was he who had asked God to provide the life force. In truth, the four men, who just the night before had been friends, were now sworn enemies, each one claiming ownership of this thing of beauty.

And so, because they could not decide who owned the stunningly mute female they made for the nearest town where they sought out the judge. Unfortunately the judge and the town's people simply thought they were fools and so sent them to see the king. Again, the king, thinking them to be fools sent them to the Sufi master who this time took all five out to see the Tree of Knowledge and with an assembled audience began to ask the tree for its wisdom. No sooner had the Sufi begun to speak than the tree opened up before them and as if by magic the young lady walked towards it and was swallowed whole. They never saw her again.

She returned to the place from whence she came, just as we all shall. It is the unity of the cycle itself. Not only are we part of the whole whilst in this part of the cycle or that part of the cycle; we are the One before and after and always shall be. As cosmic dust, solar rays and universal energy feed our planet and us, so too shall we ourselves return to cosmic dust, solar rays and universal energy one day and the fact is we never left. There is no tomorrow, no yesterday, neither exist. The only place in time and space that exists is now and that is a slice through the whole.

We are no different to that wooden woman. We came from the One into the One and so we are the One. Who is it that thinks they can form us, dress us and then give us life? Nobody owns us. To own is an anagram of now and in the now we exist. Your family, your town, your school, your employer or even your political or religious leaders – they all claim ownership at one time or another. And yet not one of them owns you just because they taught you, gave you life, gave you reason, clothed you or employed you. No ruler rules you. You are equal to everybody and everything else and no matter what another gives you it does not empower them above you.

Be strong, for you are the one.

# # #

International Best-Selling Author, Lecturer, Presenter and Director, Philip Gardiner was once a marketing expert and company owner, spending his days advising others. Then he made a discovery and re-wrote history with his international best-selling book, *The Serpent Grail*, now being translated into dozens of languages. In *Secrets of the Serpent,* the book and DVD, Gardiner unraveled the sacred past and explained how serpent worship was actually global with the same rituals and beliefs – thus radically altering our historical perspective. He quickly moved on and released *Gnosis: The Secret of Solomon's Temple Revealed* as both a book and DVD to high industry acclaim with hundreds of rave reviews for his presentation and directing style. Next he unpicked the complex tale of the Ark of the Covenant, coming under fire, met up with secret and elusive brotherhoods and scientifically re-dated the Shroud of Turin in his book and DVD, *The Ark, The Shroud and Mary*. Following on from these he undertook research into life after death in *Gateways to the Otherworld*, uncovered the secrets of James Bond and Ian Fleming in *The Bond Code* and analyzed several great characters from history in *What Wise Men Do*. His latest book, *Delusion*, will go deep into the mind of mankind and show how we delude ourselves and others.

In the midst of all this research, writing and directing, Gardiner has appeared on over 400 television and radio shows across the world from the *History Channel's* documentary *Freemasonry*, to *Fox News, Bridging Heaven and Earth, The Hilly Rose Show* and many more. He has lectured from Australia to England and from the USA to France. He hosts the television show, *Gardiner's World*, in the UK and has made several award-winning documentaries including *The Extraordinary Voyages of Jules Verne.*

Philip Gardiner's website is www.gardinersworld.com

The Ancient Code and the Stellar Origins of Consciousness

By Mitchell E. Gibson

In ancient times, mankind often looked to the heavens for guidance, inspiration, and worship. The stars were said to be the true home of the human consciousness. The physical structure of the stars were said to be inextricably linked to our destiny. The brightest stars were given names and the visible patterns created by the stars in the night sky that were called constellations. These names were often associated with living beings, gods, animals, and other important symbols connected to human life. The constellations were said to hold power over human consciousness, behavior, and daily life. To this day, almost every major newspaper in the world prints a brief horoscope, a daily column dedicated to the connection of daily human life with the stars.

Why do we maintain such a tenacious fascination with the stars? Is there a connection between human consciousness and the stars that transcends astrology and ancient mythology? In my work as a psychiatrist, I have studied medicine, astrology, metaphysics, quantum and classical physics, and human neuro-anatomy. One of the main reasons that I entered into the field of psychiatry was my fascination with the phenomenon of human consciousness. I wanted to know what it was, where it originated, how it was maintained, and how it evolved. Curiously, science has no clue as to the origins of consciousness, human or otherwise.

This fact may come as a surprise to many. Certainly, it was a huge surprise to me. After 25 years of analysis, dissection, clinical interview, and research into the phenomenon of consciousness, I never saw a memory. I never touched a thought or an emotion. I learned what other scientists have learned; the enigma of human consciousness is one of the greatest mysteries remaining in science. How can we understand this mystery better?

The mystery is human consciousness and how--or even whether--it arises out of our fleshy brains. How does it happen that billions of nerve cells collaborate in an organ no bigger than half a football, allowing us not only to navigate intricate math equations and entertain elaborate thoughts, but to observe ourselves as we perform such functions, to feel exquisite emotions that a computer couldn't begin to comprehend? More importantly, how does consciousness evolve?

My insight into the evolution of human consciousness and the stars came as many other intuitive connections in human thought have arisen, through a dream. In this dream, I found myself standing in a large parking lot near an apartment complex. Standing next to me were four individuals that I did not know. Curiously however, they were glowing with a light that seemed to emanate from within. There were three males and one female. As I stared at them, they seemed to be aware of my discomfort and gradually ceased their display of self-luminosity. The female in the group approached me after a couple of minutes, hugged me, and introduced herself as Castor.

She then pointed to the remaining trio of males and introduced them as Aldebaran, Sirius, and Betelgeuse. The all smiled, hugged me fondly, and began walking toward the apartments nearby. I asked;

"Where are you going?"

Castor turned, laughed softly and replied;

"We are going to help one of you evolve."

The group then turned and resumed their trek toward the apartments. I had no clue what she meant by her reply. From my study of astrology, I recognized each of their names. They were all the names of stars.

Puzzled, I scratched my head, turned and followed behind them. Not wanting to appear more stupid than I already felt, after a few moments, I gathered up enough courage to ask another question.

"Evolve into what?"

This time, the one who identified himself as Betelgeuse patted me on the shoulder, looked me in the eye, smiled and said;

"A star my good man, just like we always do."

The next thing I remember, we disappeared in a flash of light and reappeared on a tall hillside overlooking a cliff. I could hear the ocean waves crashing beneath our feet and I could clearly smell the salt spray of the water rising up from the surf.

I noticed however that this time there was a new addition to the group. The sixth person was a tall quiet young man who seemed to be oblivious to the true intentions of the group. He seemed to be taking the entire proceeding on faith.

In turn, each member of the group touched him on the shoulder. A visible bolt of energy erupted from each person and flowed into the man. He shuddered and seemed to stagger briefly. After they touched him, each of the individuals vanished in a flash of light.

The last to approach him was Castor. She kissed him lovingly, held his hand, and touched him lightly on the forehead. After her touch, the man began to glow brightly. Castor looked at the man and spoke softly.

"Your new name will be Michol."

Michol then levitated off the ground and soon his body became too bright for me to gaze upon. Castor followed suit and the two of them shone with a light many times brighter than the Sun. I could feel the warmth and intensity of the light even in the dream. In an instant, I stood alone in the field gazing up at the night sky. Before I awoke, I heard an echo resonating deep within the field that seemed to emanate from high above. The echo repeated one word;

"remember ... remember ... remember ... remember ..."

During my residency in psychiatry, I experienced a series of visions that began shortly after I learned to meditate while looking at the Sun. In the visions,

I met a being who identified himself as the Egyptian God Thoth. For the next two years, Thoth, who actually preferred to be called Djanti, instructed me in the arts of astrology, medicine, sacred geometry, and astral travel. I wrote about these experiences in a book entitled *Your Immortal Body of Light*. (1)

One of the concepts that Thoth explained to me that seemed exceptionally ludicrous at the time, was that human consciousness and solar consciousness were linked. In other words, the thoughts, feelings, and emotions experienced by humans were tied to an epiphenomenon of Higher Mind. Thoth's consciousness existed as a continuum of consciousness that extended into the third dimension, where it connected to my mind, and outward into the higher dimensions of reality where my conscious mind could not reach. He explained that when I meditated while looking at the Sun, for a brief time, my field of human consciousness extended into his field of higher consciousness. During that moment of contact, we communicated.

The idea that humans communicate with stars is quite old. The idea that humans descend from stars is even older. Does human consciousness have the capacity to evolve into something higher? Is the secret to that evolution contained within an ancient code hidden within astrology and metaphysics?

At first glance, the human body would seem to have nothing in common with a star. Oddly enough, nothing could be further from the truth. One of the most familiar characteristics of stars is the emission of light.

1. **Stars emit light.**

Recent studies in human photobiology reveal that human beings emit detectable amounts of photons from the body. DNA has been shown to both emit and absorb light.

All living plants and animals possess faint bio-luminescent properties and glow in the small and compartmentalized spectrum of visible light.

Human hands glow, but fingernails release the most light, according to a recent study that found all parts of the hand emit detectable levels of light. The findings support prior research that suggested most living things, including plants, release light. Since disease and illness appear to affect the strength and pattern of the glow, the discovery might lead to less invasive ways of diagnosing patients. (2)

Mitsuo Hiramatsu, a scientist at the Central Research Laboratory at Hamamatsu Photonics in Japan, who led the research, told Discovery News that the hands are not the only parts of the body that shine light by releasing photons, or tiny, energized increments of light.

"Not only the hands, but also the forehead and bottoms of our feet emit photons," Hiramatsu said, and added that in terms of hands "the presence of photons means that our hands are producing light all of the time."

The light is invisible to the naked eye, so Hiramatsu and his team used a powerful photon counter to "see" it.

The detector found that fingernails release 60 photons per second, fingers release 40 photons per second, and the palms are the dimmest of all, with 20 photons per second measured.

The findings are published in the current *Journal of Photochemistry* and *Photobiology B: Biology*.

Hiramatsu is not certain why fingernails light up more than the other parts of the hand, but he said, "It may be because of the optical window property of fingernails," meaning that the fingernail works somewhat like a prism to scatter light.

To find out what might be creating the light in the first place, he and colleague Kimitsugu Nakamura had test subjects hold plastic bottles full of hot or cold water before their hand photons were measured. The researchers also pumped nitrogen or oxygen gas into the dark box where the individuals placed their hands as they were being analyzed.

Warm temperatures increased the release of photons, as did the introduction of oxygen. Rubbing mineral oil over the hands also heightened light levels.

Based on those results, the scientists theorize the light "is a kind of chemical luminescence," a luminescence based on chemical reactions, such as those that make fireflies glow. The researchers believe 40 percent of the light results from the chemical reaction that constantly occurs as skin within the hand reacts with oxygen.

Since mineral oil, which permeates into the skin, heightens the light, they also now think 60 percent of the glow may result from chemical reactions that take place inside the skin.

Fritz-Albert Popp, a leading world expert on biologically related photons at The International Institute of Biophysics in Germany, agrees with the findings and was not surprised by them.

Popp told *Discovery News*, "One may find clear correlations to kind and degree (type and severity) of diseases."

Popp and his team believe the light from the forehead and the hands pulses out with the same basic rhythms, but that these pulses become irregular in unhealthy people. A study he conducted on a muscular sclerosis patient seemed to validate the theory.

Both he and Hiramatsu hope future studies will reveal more about human photon emissions, which could lead to medical diagnosis applications. (2)

2. **Stars generate a strong electromagnetic field around themselves.**

The human body also generates an electromagnetic field of energy around itself. The human body is made up of ions and charged particles. As such, the body is a highly charged object. Charged objects set up weak electromagnetic fields that are subjected to the earth's magnetic field.

The charged particles within the body react to the energy generated by the earth itself. Scientists have discovered that we do emit a range of electromagnetic radiation. These energies consist of infrared, ultraviolet, visible light, and certain types of radioactive energy. All of these energies are found within stars. The electromagnetic energy generated by the body is weak but can be measured.

3. Stars are a storehouse of rare-earth and heavy earth elements.

Every molecule in our bodies contains matter that once was subjected to the tremendous temperatures and pressures at the centre of a star. This is where the iron in our red blood cells originated. The oxygen we breathe, the carbon and nitrogen in our tissues, and the calcium in our bones, also were formed through the fusion of smaller atoms at the centre of a star.

Terrestrial ores containing uranium, plutonium, lead, and many other massive atoms were formed in a supernova explosion - the self-destruction of a star in which a sun's mass is hurled into space at huge velocity. In fact, most of the matter on Earth and in our bodies originated during one or more of these catastrophic events!"

The late astronomer Carl Sagan made a profoundly enigmatic statement during one of his lectures,

"We are star stuff."

While hydrogen, helium and lithium were produced during the Big Bang, all heavier chemical elements result from nuclear reactions in the interiors of stars. When stars die in one of the supernova explosions just mentioned, heavy-element enriched matter is dispersed into surrounding space and will later be incorporated in the next generations of stars. In fact, the gold, which people wear as jewelry, was produced in an exploding star and deposited in the interstellar cloud from which the Sun and its planets were later formed.

Thus, the older a star is, the lower its content of heavy elements like iron and other metals. Measurements have shown that old stars that are members of large agglomerations known as globular clusters are normally quite "metal-poor:" their metal-content ranges down to about 1/200 of that of the Sun - in which these metals constitute only 2% of the total mass, the rest being still in the form of hydrogen and helium. Our Sun is rich in heavy earth and platinum group elements.

The human body contains a large number of platinum group and heavy earth elements. Gold, platinum, rhodium, iridium, iron, nickel, copper, titanium, tine indium, and dozens of other heavy elements that first formed within stars may be found in the human body. The human brain is more than 5% rhodium and iridium by dry weight alone. Since we apparently share some important physical, chemical and energetic characteristics with the stars, how can we use this information to advance our understanding of the connection of human consciousness to the stars.

Perhaps quantum physics gives us the first clue to this mysterious link to our evolution. One of the strangest but most verifiable predictions of Einstein's theory of relativity was quantum entanglement.

Entanglement is a term used in quantum theory to describe the way that particles of energy/matter can become correlated to predictably interact with each other regardless of how far apart they are. (3)

Particles, such as photons and electrons, that have interacted with each other retain a type of connection and can be entangled with each other in pairs, in the process known as correlation. Knowing the spin state of one entangled particle - whether the direction of the spin is up or down - allows one to know that the spin of its mate is in the opposite direction.

Even more amazing is the knowledge that, due to the phenomenon of superposition, the measured particle has no single spin direction before being measured, but is simultaneously in both a spin-up and spin-down state. The spin state of the particle being measured is decided at the time of measurement and communicated to the correlated particle, which simultaneously assumes the opposite spin direction to that of the measured particle.

Quantum entanglement allows photons and electrons that are separated by incredible distances to interact with each other immediately, in a communication that is not limited to the speed of light. No matter how great the distance between the correlated particles, they will remain entangled as long as they are isolated. At the time of the Big Bang, all of our atoms were mingled.

Entanglement is a real phenomenon (Einstein called it "spooky action at a distance"), which has been demonstrated repeatedly through experimentation. The mechanism behind it cannot, as yet, be fully explained by any theory. One proposed theory suggests that all particles on earth were once compacted tightly together and, as a consequence, maintain a connectedness. Much current research is focusing on how to harness the potential of entanglement in developing systems for quantum cryptography and quantum computing. (3)

In 1997, Nicholas Gisin and colleagues at the University of Geneva used entangled photons to enable simple - but instantaneous - communication over a distance of seven miles. Scientifically, we can demonstrate that photons and electrons can communicate instantaneously over distance regardless of how far apart they are. We know that our bodies are filled with atoms, electrons, and photons that were once part of the stars that now hover above us in the heavens. The heavy elements within the brain once incubated within the core of giant stellar bodies. (4)

Do we maintain a connection with the stars through an as yet undiscovered epiphenomenon related to quantum entanglement?

Many ancient cultures maintained that the Sun and the stars held the key to man's higher evolution. Solar worship was the mainstay of many highly developed cultures for thousands of years. The ancient Egyptians, Incans, Mayans, Indonesians, Chinese, Hindu, Aztec, and Japanese were but a few cultures that held Solar deities in high esteem. As a matter of fact, evidence of Solar worship has been found on every continent on earth. Many of these same cultures also worshipped the stars themselves and built elaborate temples to track their movements over time. The Great Pyramids of Egypt have been recently shown to accurately track the movements of the stars in the constellation Orion. Why did our ancestors go to such lengths to maintain a connection to the stars?

In the book, *Your Immortal Body of Light,* Thoth outlines an astonishing series of statements related to this question. He proposed that I consider the possibility that the human form is a descendant form of life that began first within the stars. (1)

During one of my out of body travels with him, he showed me how to project my consciousness into the Sun itself. On one particular Solar journey, I saw a field of human forms sleeping within what appeared to be a sort of embryonic pod. There were millions and millions of these pods. Thoth explained that humanity has the capacity to evolve beyond the physical form and transfer his consciousness into one of the slumbering energetic forms seen in the pods.

When one researches the overall goal of the solar practices performed by the ancients, a peculiar fact emerges. Their goal in this work was not simply to worship the Sun and stars. In almost every instance, I discovered that the true goal of these solar practices was the apotheosis; that is, the complete transformation of man into a being of light.

In the last stage of solar enlightenment, the human body itself is changed from flesh into light. Through the process of transubstantiation of the flesh, blood, skin, and bone, one actually becomes a being made of light. This Light Body is generally accepted to be an immortal and indestructible Form by all accounts.

In the Judeo-Christian tradition, this body is called the "resurrection body" or the "glorified body." Saint Paul called it the "celestial body" or the "spiritual body."

In Sufism, it is called "the most sacred body" and the "supracelestial body." In Taoism, it is called "the diamond body," and those few humans who have attained it are called "the immortals." In Tibetan Buddhism, it is called "the light body." In Tantrism and various yoga systems it is called "the vajra body" and "the adamantine body." In ancient Egypt, it was called "the luminous being." Sri Aurobindo, a great Indian teacher and mystic, stated that "divine body" is the ultimate stage of human evolution. He felt that a deathless condition resulting from transubstantiation of the fleshly body could be attained by personal effort, meditation, and divine grace.

The seeds of this immortal form are said to exist within each of us. One may understand the analogy as a metaphor. The butterfly emerges from the caterpillar, and the two look nothing alike. The caterpillar contains all the information within its genome necessary for its transformation into a butterfly. In the process, there is a complete transubstantiation of its fleshly body into something totally unlike its birth form. According to the ancients, all humans possess this transformative ability.

Only three percent of the three billion base pair genome of our DNA encodes the physical body. Ninety-seven percent of our three billion DNA base pairs appear to be totally inactive during the normal course of human life. Is it possible that the vast dormant potential represented by these billions of base pairs forms the basis for the formation of a higher state of physical expression for the body?

Is it possible that the human body acts as a cocoon for a higher, more complex, longer-lived form which has the potential for immortality? In the process of my research, I found a number of well-documented historical cases that seemed to bear out the reality of a multiplicity of spiritual forms, including the Light Body, that are connected to the human body in everyday human experiences.

In 1999, David Steindl-Rast, a Benedictine monk, proposed investigating the "rainbow body," a phenomenon in which the corpses of highly developed spiritual individuals reputedly vanished within days of death. Brother David had been fascinated by the stories that he had heard about this remarkable phenomenon from several of his colleagues who lived in Tibet. He contacted Marilyn Schlitz, the Director of Research at the Institute of Noetic Sciences, (IONS). She was very enthusiastic about the idea and invited him to discuss it with her further.

In a new joint initiative with the Esalen Institute, the IONS was expanding its research on "metanormal capacities." These capacities encompassed behaviors, experiences, and bodily changes that challenge our understanding of ordinary human functioning. They also raise crucial questions about the developmental potential of human beings.

In 1999, he decided to explore the strange phenomenon of the rainbow body and a possible connection to the resurrection of Jesus. He sent a fax to a friend in Switzerland, who was a Zen Buddhist teacher. The phenomenon occurred frequently among certain Zen Buddhist sects and Steindl-Rast hoped that his friend might know of some practitioners who could provide more information.

Two days later, he received a fax stating that a Tibetan monk had unexpectedly approached him. When the rainbow body was mentioned, the Tibetan said, "It happened to one of my teachers just recently, and a famous lama who witnessed the events wrote an account about them." At this point, Steindl-Rast contacted Father Francis Tiso, an ordained Roman Catholic priest who has studied ten languages, including Tibetan. Francis Tiso holds the office of Canon in the Cathedral of St. Peter and is a parochial vicar.

Steindl-Rast knew that Father Tiso occasionally went to Tibet and asked him if he was planning to travel there in the near future. As fortune would have it,

Father Tiso was leaving for Tibet that day. Steindl-Rast asked if he would stop in Switzerland and interview the Tibetan. Despite the short notice, Tiso took a detour to Switzerland, and thus the research journey began.

Through his Swiss contact, Tiso received the name of the monk whose body had vanished after his death. His name was Khenpo A-chos. He was a Gelugpa monk from Kham, Tibet who died in 1998. Tiso was able to locate the village, situated in a remote area where Khenpo A-chos had his hermitage. He then went to the village and conducted taped interviews with eyewitnesses to Khenpo A-chos' death. He also spoke to many people who had known him.

Tiso interviewed Lama Norta, a nephew of Khenpo Achos; Lama Sonam Gyamtso, a young disciple; and Lama A-chos, a dharma friend of the late Khenpo A-chos. They described the following:

A few days before Khenpo A-chos died, a rainbow appeared directly above his hut. After he died, there were dozens of rainbows in the sky. Khenpo A-chos died lying on his right side. He wasn't sick; there appeared to be nothing wrong with him, and he was reciting the mantra OM MANI PADME HUM over and over. According to the eyewitnesses, after his breath stopped his flesh became kind of pinkish. One person said it turned brilliant white. All said it started to shine.

Lama A-chos suggested wrapping his friend's body in a yellow robe, the type all Gelug monks wear. As the days passed, they maintained that they could see, through the robe that his bones and his body were shrinking. They also heard beautiful, mysterious music coming from the sky, and they smelled perfume.

After seven days, they removed the yellow cloth, and no body remained. These eye witnesses claim that Khenpo A-chos had totally disappeared. Lama Norta and a few other individuals claimed that after his death Khenpo A-chos appeared to them in visions and dreams.

Francis Tiso remarked that one of his most intriguing interviews was with Lama A-chos. He told Tiso that when he died he too would manifest the rainbow body. "He showed us two photographs taken of him in the dark, and in these photographs his body radiated rays of light."

Because Lama A-chos emphasized that it was possible to manifest the rainbow body while still alive, not just in death, Tiso plans to return to Tibet with professional camera equipment to try to photograph this radiating light. This is by no means an isolated incident. Francis Tiso is a graduate of the Harvard School of Divinity and holds a doctorate degree from Columbia University. His research is painstaking and meticulous. (5)

The process of solar body development requires the use of solar mantras, the intake of starlight and sunlight into the body, and the use of certain special rare earth elements that are taken into the body via sacred dietary rituals. The solar mantras vary from culture to culture but are designed to align the consciousness of the aspirant with the energies resonated by the Sun and stars. The ancient Solar Adepts believed that the stars radiated a special energy frequency that could be likened unto a song or signature voice.

Recent discoveries in stellar seismography have revealed that each star radiates a complex series of radio waves that may be translated into sound. These sounds resonate throughout the body of the star very much like a heartbeat. Each star has its own characteristic heartbeat. The more evolved the star, the more distinct and resonant its heartbeat becomes. Science has once again confirmed a major tenet of the ancient code.

The sound resonance energy of many stars has been recorded. Each of these recordings captures photons of energy from the star in the form of sound. Think about it for a moment, what would happen to human consciousness if it were exposed to the energy resonance of an ancient Giant Star. Remember, each of us is literally filled with heavy elements that are derived directly from stars. These elements did not come from the earth. Since the brain, nervous system, organs, bones, teeth etc. are all filled with these elements, how would they react to this type of resonant stimulation?

Is it possible to awaken dormant DNA structures within the body that await this type of resonance from the stars? Many solar cultures believed that the stars were conscious entities that regularly communicated with humans via super-conscious phenomena that we could learn to harness and master. The most powerful of these stellar conscious entities were called gods and were worshipped for their wisdom, knowledge, and superior intelligence. The combination of stellar sound resonance technology, light body development, and solar meditation may well hold the key for man's higher development. In our rapidly changing world, we have seen that man's ability to create technological advances often far outstrips his ability to evolve physically and spiritually.

The ancients understood that man's survival and higher evolution were linked to the stars. Modern science is rapidly confirming much of what ancient science and mythology believed. Perhaps, our study of the ancient codes related to the stars and the Sun holds a treasure trove of information yet to be discovered about our futures and our destiny.

The consciousness and power of a star compared to that of one human would be immeasurable. Would it be possible for a star to take human form and interact with a human? I say yes, if that human were prepared to accept the phone call.

We are made from the dust of the stars. I believe that the phenomenon of human consciousness is linked to the epiphenomenon of stellar consciousness that resides within the stars. This link is strengthened through the energies, elements, and fields of consciousness that we share with the stars. The future expansion and evolution of human consciousness resides in our comprehension of this link and the power hidden there.
When I reflect on the dream that inspired me to investigate our deeper links to the stars, I marvel at the simplicity of the message.

"remember … remember … remember …"

Mitchell Earl Gibson, MD
June 25, 2009

(1) *Your Immortal Body of Light*: Mitchell Earl Gibson MD
Reality Press, August 2006. www.reality-entertainment.com/books.htm
(2) *Ultra-weak photon emission from human hand*: *Influence of temperature and oxygen concentration on emission:* Kimitsugu Nakamura and Mitsuo Hiramatsu, Electron Tube Division, Hamamatsu Photonics K.K., Toyooka, Japan Central Research Laboratory, Hamamatsu Photonics K.K., Hirakuchi, Hamakita 434-8601, Japan
(3) Center for Quantum Computations: *Introduction to Quantum Entanglement.* Leah Henderson and Vlatko Vedra. Pages 1-3.

(4) *Quantum cryptography* (2008), Nicolas Gisin, Gregoire Ribordy, Wolfgang Tittel, Hugo Zbinden
(5) *The Human Body of Light*: Mitchell Earl Gibson MD
Tybro Publications, August 2008. www.tybro.com

#

Dr. Mitchell Earl Gibson is a board-certified forensic psychiatrist, author, and public speaker. He received his medical degree from the University of North Carolina at Chapel Hill, completing his residency training at the Albert Einstein Medical Center in Philadelphia. During his last year of residency, Dr. Gibson served as Chief Resident in Psychiatry and received the Albert Einstein Foundation Research Award for his work in Sleep Disorders. He is a former Chief of Staff at the East Valley Camelback Hospital in Mesa Arizona and a Clinical Professor of Medicine and Psychiatry at the Midwestern College of Medicine.

Dr. Gibson has worked as a mental health consultant for Forest Pharmaceuticals, Smith, Kline, and Beecham, Bristol Myers Squibb, Intel, Samaritan Health Services, Essence, Upscale, Ebony, and First for Women, and The Arizona Republic. He has lectured extensively throughout the United States, Canada, and Europe as a noted public speaker on various topics including creating mental health without medication, the spiritual causes of mental illness, human potential, the mind-body-spirit connection, and creativity enhancement. His profound experiences documented in *Your Immortal Body of Light* have led him on a healing path outside of traditional medicine. Dr. Gibson teaches a spiritual development course and conducts seminars on the topics presented in his book.

The Sacred Bee in Ancient Egypt

By Andrew Gough

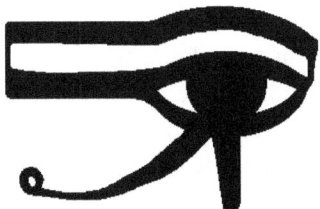

The Birth of Bee Veneration

The 21st century has seen a revival of interest in bees and an increased appreciation for their contribution to society, due sadly, to the fact that they were dying, and their demise would dramatically worsen an already depressed and still weakening world economy. There would simply be no replacing the earth's most industrious pollinator of plants and trees - a vital function for life on our planet – and producers of medicinal and health food products, such as honey. For the longest time, the life affirming attributes of bees and their by-products was well understood by society at large, and care of the hive nurtured, rather than exploited, the bee.

The ancient Egyptians understood the unique value that bees provide and incorporated them into their everyday life, and religion. They did not invent bee veneration; they inherited it, and all indications suggest that the tradition dates back thousands of years. Incredibly, bees over 100 million years old have been discovered in amber, frozen in time, as if immortalized in their own honey. The Greeks called amber Electron, associated with the Sun God Elector, who was known as the awakener, a term also given to honey - which resembles amber – a regenerative substance revered across the ancient world. This association led to the bees' illustrious status amongst ancient man, exalting their fossilized remains over the preserved vestiges of all other insects.

Prehistory is full of clues that hint at ancient man's obsession with bees, but they have largely gone unnoticed. In the Cave of the Spider near Valencia in Spain, a 15,000-year-old painting depicts a determined looking figure risking his life to extract honey from a precarious cliff-side beehive. Honey hunting represents one of man's earliest hunter / gatherer pursuits – its very difficulty hinting at the genesis of the bee's adoration in prehistory. And of course, it was the bee that led ancient shamans to the plants whose hallucinogens transported their consciousness into the spirit world of the gods. Curiously, recent research has revealed that the sound of a bee's hum has been observed during moments of state changes in human consciousness, including individuals who have experienced alleged UFO abductions, apparitions, and near death experiences. Was this phenomenon known by the ancients and believed to have been one of the elements that made the bee special?

In Anatolia, a 10,000-year-old statue of the Mother Goddess adorned in a yellow and orange Beehive-style tiara has led scholars to conclude that the Mother Goddess had begun to morph into the Queen Bee, or bee goddess, around this time. At the Neolithic settlement of Catal Huyuk, rudimentary images of bees dating to 6540 BC are painted above the head of a Goddess in the form of a halo and beehives are stylistically portrayed on the walls of sacred temples. Not surprisingly, it was the Sumerians who soon emerged as the forefathers of organized bee keeping. Mesopotamia - modern day Iraq – flourished from the early sixth century BC and is known as the cradle of civilization, and it is here that the Sumerians invented Apitherapy, or the medical use of bee products such as honey, pollen, royal jelly, propolis and venom.

Sumerian reliefs depicting the adoration of extraordinary winged figures have often been interpreted by alternative history writers as proof of extraterrestrial intervention. In the context of the benefits of beekeeping, might they actually portray the veneration of bees? Significantly, the images gave rise to the dancing goddess motif; a female dancer with her arms arched over her head that scholars believe represents a bee goddess priestess or shaman. The motif, which would become central to Egyptian symbolism, appears to allude to the bee's unique ability to communicate through dance; the waggle dance as it is known, or the ability to locate food up to 3 miles from home and return to communicate its whereabouts to the hive through dance, sort of prehistoric satellite navigation.

So, society had discovered the immense value that bees provide, ten thousand years ago or more, back in the mist of prehistory. As life along the River Nile evolved and Dynastic rule in ancient Egypt slowly developed, the seeds of bee veneration had already been sown. But the tradition was about to be embraced like never before, or since.

Genesis of the Bee in Ancient Egypt

The ancient Egyptians shared many similarities with the Sumerians, including the veneration of bees. Sophisticated apiculture, or the organized craft of beekeeping, was practiced in Egypt for thousands of years. According to bee expert Eva Crane, whose authoritative book, *The World History of Beekeeping and Honey Hunting* (1999) remains the primary reference work for the genre: "beekeeping was very important before 3000 BC, especially in the Delta." In other words, the agricultural, nutritional, medicinal and ritual value of the bee, and its by-products, was important in Egypt from pre-dynastic times onwards.

Egypt's fascination with the bee from the earliest of epochs is reinforced by the fact that King Menes, founder of the First Egyptian Dynasty, was bestowed with the office of "Beekeeper;" a title ascribed to all subsequent Pharaohs, and the King's administration had a special position created called the "Sealer of the Honey," while the Kings of Upper and Lower Egypt bore the title "he who belongs to the sedge and the bee." An image of the bee was even positioned next to each Pharaoh's cartouche.

Intriguingly, Northern Egypt - the land stretching from the Delta to Memphis was known as "Ta-Bitty," or "the land of the bee." Similarly in the Bible, Yahweh promises to bring the Israelites out of slavery in Egypt into a land flowing with milk and honey. Poetically, later civilizations referred to this as a sort of mythical utopia; a bountiful, abundant and fertile region, reminiscent of the Mother Goddess herself. Similarly, at the temple of Dendera an inscription recounts how Osiris, consort of the goddess Isis, emulated the bee and provided instructions for knowing the "hsp," or sacred garden of the bee in the other world - a domain believed to contain the tree of the golden apples of immortality.

Egyptologist Wallis Budge (1857–1934) translated the sacred Egyptian text, *Book of Opening the Mouth*, and in doing so provided insight that confirmed the bees' importance in Egyptian mythology. One phrase of the ancient text simply read: "The Bee, giving him protection, they make him to exist," while another states: "Going about as a bee, thou seest all the goings about of thy father." The later may in fact refer to the Ka, or an individual's soul - or double, which is nurtured after death. Albeit cryptic to our modern ears, these early references to bees confirm that in Egypt, the diminutive insect was held sacred since the very earliest time.

In addition to the *Book of Opening the Mouth*, Egyptian mythology contains countless references to bees, including the belief that they were formed from the tears of the most important god in its pantheon, RA. The ancient writings of Am-Tuat (the Otherworld) explains:

"This god cries out to their souls after he hath entered the city of the gods who are on their sand, and there are heard the voices of those who are shut in this circle which are like the hum of many bees of honey when their souls cry out to Ra."

And similarly, the *Salt Magical Papyrus* states:

"When RA weeps again and the water which flows from his eyes upon the ground turns into working bees. They work in flowers and trees of every kind and wax and honey come into being."

The bee's association with the tears of RA is interesting, for the image, or ideogram, of the bee has been interpreted by Egyptologists to represent honey, and its eyes to convey the verb "to see." Many have studied its meaning, such as the Egyptologist Sir Alan Gardiner (1879 – 1963), who featured the bee in his book *Egyptian Grammar*. So did the German Egyptologist Kurt Sethe (1869 – 1934), who believed the Egyptians had forgotten the original word for bee. Similarly, the Egyptologist Hermann Grapow (1885 – 1967) felt that the bee's title was completely "unreadable." While Egyptologists agree that the bee was sacred in Egypt, they have yet to ascertain, let alone agree, the symbol's true meaning.

Bees are portrayed on the walls of Egyptian tombs and offerings of honey were routinely presented to the most important Egyptian deities. Indeed, honey was the "nectar of the gods," and like the Sumerians before them, Egyptian physicians relied on its medicinal value for many important remedies and procedures. It seems the Egyptians also practiced Apitherapy.

Egyptian medicine men were often indistinguishable from sorcerers, and beeswax was an essential ingredient in the creation of effigies used in their most sacred rituals. In her 1937 book, *The Sacred Bee*, Hilda Ransome recounts several examples, stating that "One of the earliest instances of the magical use of wax is in the *Westcar Papyrus*." Ransome recounts how a beeswax effigy of a crocodile comes alive and eats the lover of a man's wife as revenge for violating his marriage agreement.

Honey was frequently mentioned in papyri and was even a vital ingredient in Egyptian beer, linking the bee to commerce, for beer was often used as a form of wages. Further reinforcing its importance in Egyptian society – and religion - many byproducts of honey were placed next to the sarcophagi as offerings to the souls of the deceased in the afterlife. This included honeycombs, honey cakes, sealed jars of honey as well as lotus blooms. In fact, the versatile nectar was so cherished that promises of honey from husband to wife were included in many marriage contracts. Even Pharaoh traded in honey, as demonstrated by Ramses III, who offered 15 tons of it to the Nile God Hapi in the 12th Century BC.

The bee is featured prominently in many Egyptian temples, including the pillars of Karnak, the Luxor obelisk now erected on the Place de la Concorde in Paris; the 20th Dynasty sarcophagus of Rameses III; a granite statue of Rameses II; the sarcophagus of a 26th Dynasty priest, and on the Pyramid of Unas, to name but a few. It is also featured in the tomb of Pa-Ba-Sa, in Thebes, where an entire wall is decorated with rows of bees. Here a man is shown pouring honey into a pail while another is kneeling and praying before a pyramid of honeycombs. Similarly the many facets of honey industry are depicted on the wall of the tomb of Rekh-Mi-Re, including images showing how the combs were extracted from the hives with the aid of smoke, the baking of honey cakes and the filling and sealing of jars with honey. And in the Egyptian Delta, in the ancient Temple of Tanis – believed to have once housed the Ark of the Covenant, the bee was its first and most important ideogram. In fact, the bee is even featured on the most famous of Egyptian stele; the Rosetta Stone.

The Lost Wadis of the Bee Goddess

An intriguing source for the genesis of bee symbolism in Egyptian mythology is the Eastern Egyptian Desert (EED) – a desolate expanse of Wadis stretching eastward from Luxor in the west, to the Red Sea in the east. The seldom-visited territory is renowned for its pre-dynastic rock art, etched on barren cliff sides and isolated rock faces. The region has quietly emerged as a leading candidate for Egypt's pre-dynastic origins, and may hold vital clues as to the genesis of bee symbolism in Egyptian society.

The importance of EED rock art as an indicator of pre-dynastic Egyptian settlement was first observed by two pioneering Egyptologists in the early part of the 20th century; Arthur Weigall in 1907 and Hans Winkler in 1936. The region was later popularized by Egyptologist and chronology revisionist David Rohl, whose 1998 book *Legend; The Genesis of Civilization*, and subsequent catalogue of EED rock art, revivified the debate over Egypt's origins and underscored the valley's importance in pre-dynastic studies.

The essence of Rohl's hypothesis is that EED rock art depicts the migration of a people who transported their boats from Mesopotamia across the eastern desert and into the Nile Valley, where they ultimately settled and founded the pre-dynastic Egyptian civilization. In this scenario, the terraced Step Pyramid at Saquara, along with its accompanying niched-façade temples, pillars and walls, is thought to have been influenced by earlier Sumerian Ziggurats, such as the one at the ancient city of Ur. Another respected Egyptologist, Dr. Toby Wilkinson from Cambridge University, also wrote of the importance of the EED in his book; *Genesis of the Pharaohs* (2001). I toured the region with both men in 1999 and found its evocative rock art to be magical, mysterious, and well worth the often difficult journey.

The EED rock art features two images of relevance in our analysis, each occurring with regularity in the Wadi's leading westward to the Nile Valley. The first is an exalted looking figure with exaggerated plume-like decorations, as featured in countless Egyptian reliefs and paintings. The plumed figure appears in both male and female form, and is usually depicted standing in a boat. The unusual lines extending upwards from the main figures' heads, recall the antenna of the bee while hinting at the shape of the plumes that would characterize the headdress of Egyptian Kingship for thousands of years to come. They also recall the god Amun, who is frequently shown with two tall plumes rising on top of a crown. Thousands of years later, Roman Catholic Popes would feature the bee as an emblem of their papacy while adorning themselves with a headdress that was indistinguishable from that worn by Amun, and especially Osiris, the ancient Egyptian god of the afterlife, rebirth and fertility. Might the genesis of that symbolism have been born in the EED, and if so, was it inspired by bee veneration?

The other image of note is the Dancing Goddess motif, a woman with her hands bowed over her head just as the bee Goddess had been depicted in Sumerian and Central European reliefs thousands of years earlier. The image is widespread in Egyptian mythology, although its origins remain a mystery. The abundance of Dancing Goddess images in the EED is especially intriguing, for they appear to support two different but equally interesting scenarios. Firstly, that the EED was one of the routes traveled by the Sumerians into the Nile Valley – as argued by Rohl, and secondly, that the EED was the path traveled by the forefathers of the Mormon religion; a group whose mythology is nothing if not obsessed with a legendary man-led migration of bees across the ancient world and into America – or so its modern founders claim.

Yosef Garfinkel also informs us of an intriguing observation in his 2003 book, *Dancing at the Dawn of Agriculture*;

"In the early Neolithic period of the Near East, female figures played the dominant role in dancing, and they compromise 75% of the depictions. In Predynastic Egypt, a similar, high proportion of female figures appears in the dancing scenes (ca 83%)."

Once again, this is especially interesting when we consider that the bee is the only insect that communicates with dance, and according to scholars, Dancing Goddesses represent bees – and here in the pre-dynastic EED we find a huge assortment of Dancing Goddess figures; a motif that would become widespread across all dynasties of Egyptian culture.

Yet another visual clue of the influence of the bee in Egyptian culture is the ceremonial Egyptian dress, which has certain stylistic similarities with the bee, namely the headdress, or nemes, which consists of alternating yellow and dark horizontal stripes. This visual synchronicity is discernible in many reliefs and sculptures but is perhaps best illustrated in the death mask of the 18th Dynasty Pharaoh, Tutankhamen, which famously depicts the Pharaoh adorned in alternating black and yellow stripes or bands, just like a bee. Similarly, the Egyptian deity Nut is frequently depicted in a dress woven with a honeycomb pattern that recalls the bee's home, its hive. Ultimately the notion that the sacred bee goddess inspired the dress of the Egyptian gods and royalty should not be surprising, given the adoption of the motif in earlier cultures, such as the swirling orange and yellow Beehive tiara of the 8th millennium BC Turkish bee Goddess that preceded Egyptian culture by over five thousand years – a motif agreed by scholars to represent the bee.

Once again, Marija Gimbutas provides a valuable perspective: "The image of the goddess in the shape of a bee or some other kind of insect has a very long history." With this in mind, the notion of the Mother Goddess manifest as Queen Bee is interesting, for bees are the definitive example of a true matriarchal society. The Queen Bee rules, and is viewed as the "mother" of all bees in the hive. She's fierce, and her power is absolute.

The Queen bee is developed in a pouch while the worker and drone bees gestate in the traditional 6-sided honeycomb cell, and she develops in 16 days – approximately 5 days faster than other bees. As a young bee, the Queen in waiting is fed "royal jelly" – a high protein substance derived from the heads of young Worker Bees. The young royal is groomed to become the sole, mated Queen in the hive, and is expected to kill all competitors that stand in her way. Her success as a "warrior princess" is facilitated by the fact that unlike her rivals, her training has enabled her to sting repeatedly without dying. So in effect, the Queen bee is the prototype for many of the female figures who feature so prominently in Egyptian culture, from Hatshepsut, the 5th Pharaoh of the 18th Dynasty Hatshepsut, right through to Cleopatra and all the Goddesses in between, some of which we will discuss shortly.

If the bee Goddess was a manifestation of the Mother Goddess, then we must ask; why is her symbolism not more visible in Egyptian mythology? One possibility is that the Mother Goddess manifested as a "Queen Bee" or bee Goddess, morphing into another deity altogether. Another possibility is that the tradition was later suppressed - but why?

The Bee Goddess Becomes Egyptian

There is several Egyptian deities that the Mother Goddess turned Bee Goddess may have evolved into, including the Egyptian God Min, who was known as the "Master of the Wild Bees." Min was a pre-dynastic bee master, dated to 3000 BC, or even earlier, who is traditionally depicted dressed in feathers with bee-like antenna plumes and an erect penis symbolizing fertility and regeneration – traits of bees, and his symbols include a white bull and an arrow. Although Min is a strong candidate, upon closer inspection, it appears that the Egyptian Goddess Neith is in fact the deity that the Mother Goddess turned bee Goddess morphed into, for Neith was a warrior deity also possessing fertility symbolism and virginal mother qualities; all attributes of the Mother Goddess – and the Queen bee.

Neith was an important deity from the First Dynasty (3050 – 2850 BC) whose cult was based in Sais, a town in the Western Nile Delta. Sadly, her temple is now lost from history, but fortunately some interesting accounts have survived. We are informed by the 5th century Greek Historian Herodotus, in his work Histories, that the temple had "pillars carved so as to resemble palm-trees." Herodotus also informs us that the gateway to the temple was;

"An astonishing work, far surpassing all other buildings of the same kind in both extent and height, and built with stones of rare size and excellency."

The Romans later revived the cult of Neith and reenacted rituals symbolizing her summer return – on a boat, like the bee Goddess was portrayed in the EED, as it migrated from eastern lands. In Sais, Neith was regarded as the Goddess of the "House of the Bee" and the Mother of RA; "the ruler of all." Neith's House of the bee bore a very curious inscription, indeed, as first-century historian Lucius Mestrius Plutarchus recounts:

"I am All That Has Been, That Is, and That Will Be. No mortal has yet been able to lift the veil that covers Me."

The 18th-century author and philosopher of early German Romanticism, George Philipp Friedrich von Hardenberg – more commonly known as Novalis - paid homage to the inscription in his riddle:

"There was one who arrived there. He lifted the veil of the goddess at Sais. But what did he see? Wonder above wonder, he saw himself."

Neith was known as the Veiled Goddess, and thus the reference on her temple inscription to "lifting a veil" is intriguing, for bees are often called hymenoptera, stemming from the word hymen, meaning "veil winged," representing that which concealed the holy parts of a temple, as well as the veil or hymen of a woman's reproductive organ. Only later did the veiled wing become associated with the goddess Isis.

Equally as curious, Herodotus tells us that the Egyptian god Osiris – whose many symbols included the Beehive, was buried behind the "House of the Bee," which is tantalizing on several levels. Firstly, Osiris is associated with the bee and regeneration, representing the transformation of souls in the afterlife. Secondly, the Temple of Neith is where Plato recounted the legend of Atlantis, as relayed by Egyptian priests to the Greek law-giver Solon. Validating Plato's account some 300 years later, a philosopher by the name of Crantor traveled to Sais to investigate the legend for himself. As Simon Cox and Mark Foster recount in *An A to Z of Atlantis*:

"Crantor says that he saw the columns in the temple on which the hieroglyphic inscriptions recounted the destruction of the civilization of Atlantis."

The entire legend is interesting, for the location most commonly believed by scholars to be Atlantis is a Minoan island known in ancient times as Thera, or modern day Santorini. Minoans shared many similarities with the Egyptians, including the veneration of bees – and as we shall explore shortly, both civilizations venerated bulls as an extension of their bee veneration. Although speculative, the notion of Atlantis as a centre of bull and bee worship is alluring, and based on the evidence – excitingly - not entirely unfounded.

It's worth noting that the Western Oasis of Siwa is where Alexander The Great visited the famous Oracle of Amun: the Egyptian god with the Bee antenna inspired plumes on his crown. This is particularly interesting, given the fact that Alexander's corpse was believed to have been wrapped in honey, a common custom throughout Egypt and Assyria. Once again, it is Herodotus who comments on the tradition when he reports that; "Babylonians buried their dead in honey, and had funeral lamentations like the Egyptians." Might the use of honey in ancient burials hint at the earliest forms of mummification?

The Sacred Bee and the Bull

An Egyptian monument that exhibits bee symbolism, albeit subtly, is the Saqqara step pyramid, which boasts 6 levels above ground and 1 very special level below - the Apis bull necropolis known as the Serapeum. On the most fundamental level, the step pyramid recalls the 6-sided shape of a Bee's honeycomb as well as the 6th god of the Egyptian pantheon – Asar, known also as Osiris - the god of life and death whose symbol is the Djed pillar, and who was often depicted as a "green man."

The Serapeum was discovered northwest of the Step Pyramid in 1850 by the French explorer Auguste Mariette, who became interested in Saqqara after traveling to Egypt to study Coptic texts. The story goes that he observed the head of a Sphinx protruding from the sand near the Step Pyramid, which ultimately led him to the entrance of the necropolis where he discovered a burial hall of sacred Egyptian Apis bulls; Apis, meaning "Bee" in Latin. Herodotus described the Apis bull as sacred, stating that the:

"Apis is the calf of a cow which is never afterwards able to bear young. The Egyptians say that fire comes down from heaven upon the cow, which thereupon bears Apis."

And Herodotus also distinguished between the fate of the male and female bull:

"… it was only the black bulls with special marks – a white disc between its horns being one of the most important – who were really entitled to the name Apis."

And finally, Hilda Ransome adds;

"The females, who are sacred to Isis, are thrown into the river (Nile), but the males are buried in the suburbs of the towns with one or both of their horns appearing above the surface of the ground to mark the place. When the bodies are decayed a boat comes, at an appointed time, from the island of Prosopitis, which is a portion of the Delta, and calls at the various cities in turn to collect the bones of the oxen."

The descriptions of the Apis bull are fascinating, and underscore its ritualistic significance in Egyptian religion and society. It also highlights the fact that only certain bulls were revered, namely the Apis, which was all black except for a white triangle on its forehead, and a bull with a white body and a black head called Muntu, sacred to the bee master god Min. The cult of the god Apis dates to the First Dynasty and possibly earlier, for the constellation of the Age of Taurus was first sited in 4530 BC. Like the Apis bull itself, the constellation has a distinctive triangle on its forehead, with a prominent star – Alderbaran, in the location of the "third eye," which to the esoteric world represents the 7th chakra, or the passage through the abyss and the notion of transcending time. Clearly, the Egyptians were obsessed with the veneration of the bull. The question remains, was their obsession of the bull intrinsically linked to the bee?

Egyptologists believe that the Apis bull was bestowed with the regenerative qualities of the Memphite god Ptah – the Egyptian god of reincarnation. They also believed that those who inhaled the breath of the Apis bull received the gift of prophesy, and perhaps most importantly of all, the Egyptians believed that the bull was transformed into Osiris Apis, after death. "Bee" in Latin is "Apis," which may have derived from Sipa / Asipa in Mesopotamia; Sipa meaning "Great Shepherd in the Sky" and Apis meaning Osiris. This relates to the belief that after death, the Pharaoh's soul joined Osiris as a star in the constellation of Orion. Alternatively, some believe it became a bee star in the constellation of Cancer. And of course, serendipitously, Sipa is Apis spelt backwards.

The god Apis was related to Osiris / Asar and carried the title "WHM," meaning repetition of births. It is important to note that Osiris is neither associated with regeneration - the concept of starting over at the beginning of the cosmic ladder of births - nor with reincarnation, the progression forward or backward in the cosmic ladder based on the virtue of one's actions in this life. Rather, Osiris represented the true, pre-Christian definition of resurrection, or the obtainment of total consciousness and awareness of all that has been and will be, by willingly stepping off the ladder of rebirth after death and terminating the process of reincarnation. And this required intensive preparation, clear intent and elaborate ritual.

Curiously, Osiris's birth was announced by three wise men – or stars, his flesh was symbolically eaten in the form of communion cakes and he was murdered under a full moon before being resurrected. Because of these, and other similarities with the life of Jesus Christ, Osiris is regarded by many as the archetypal savior, the supreme dying-and-rising god. Furthermore, the Qumran Essenes, which some have linked to Jesus, were believed to be "King Bees," while Jesus Christ was regarded as an Ethereal bee. And as Osiris and Jesus are linked to bees – once again the question is: by association, were bees also connected with the concept of resurrection?

The worship of the bull in ancient cultures predates its veneration in Egypt by thousands of years. In Old Europe – the South of France in particular - caves deep underground depict sacred bulls, such as the 17-foot bull painted on a wall in the "Hall of the Bull" at Lascaux. And in the "Temple of Bull Heads" at Catal Huyuk, Anatolia, bulls appear to have provided an important ritual function, as previously discussed. So might the significance of the bull be related to the bee, in each instance?

As previously noted, the bee was regarded as sacred due to its multi-purpose nectar and ability to process pollen, a substance regarded as a life-giving "dust" since time immemorial. Lands that were graced with bees flourished – those that were not frequently languished, which links it, interestingly, with myths of the Holy Grail. However, the regenerative symbolism of bees born from bulls appears to be the aspect the Egyptians revered most, for we are told that an Apis bull (again, Apis meaning "Bee" in Latin) produced 1000 bees, and that the bees represented souls. Intriguingly, the Egyptian Goddess Nut was the goddess of the sky – the domain of Bees - and keeper of the title She Who Holds a Thousand Souls, which appears to refer to the 1000 bees – or souls – that are regenerated from the body of an Apis bull.

Similarly, and even more curious is the fact that the Hebrew letter Alef | Aleph carries the meaning "thousand" and both the Proto-Sinatic Hieroglyphic and its Pro-Canaanite symbol depict a bulls head, alluding to the fact that 1000 Bees - or resurrected souls, are produced by the sacrifice of an Apis bull. Additionally, Christ - the savior archetype of Osiris, renowned for his resurrection, is written in Hebrew as "QRST" and carries the value 1000. And of course Osiris has strong links with the Bee, as we have seen. It is unclear where the number 1000 comes from, or for that matter, precisely where and how the concept originated. Nevertheless, the symbolism appears fully formed in Egyptian society from its inception, and in this context is it any wonder that bulls were held sacred? Of course bulls provided an important practical function, but could the fact that an Apis bull produced 1000 bees (or souls) have been the real reason why such an animal was held sacred in the first place, as it was 4000 years earlier in ancient Turkey and even earlier in France?

There has been a great deal of speculation about a statue of an Apis bull found in the Serapeum, particularly and the object depicted between its horns. The conventional belief is that the image represents the Solar Disc, as found between the horns of the Goddess Hathor – the patroness of Alchemy. The belief that bees and beehives represented a "library" of knowledge was quite common in the ancient world and another school of thought is that the Solar Disc represents the collective wisdom of bees in the form of a bowl of honey.

The ancient belief that bees were born of bulls leads us to suggest that the underground necropolis known as the Serapeum may have been a ritual centre of regeneration designed to recycle souls from the heads of bulls, and not simply a mausoleum for sacred Apis bulls. The reader will recall that it was a Sphinx submerged in the sand that led Mariette to unearth the Serapeum in the first place. Poetically, this account recalls an earlier passage from the works of Antigonos of Karystos, a philosopher and writer circa 250 BC who recorded a hauntingly similar custom in ancient Egypt;

"In Egypt if you bury the Ox in certain places, so that only his horns project above ground and then saw them off, they say that bees fly out; for the ox putrefies and is resolved into bees."

So, the Saqqara Serapeum may have been a ritual centre for regenerating souls via bees born of bulls. Might the Serapeum have been a centre for what later surfaced as Mithraism, an ancient mystery school with rites involving the slaughter of bulls?

At this juncture, it is worth summarizing that the Bee was the symbol of Egypt, and that Beekeeper was the title given to the Pharaoh, while honey was an offering presented to the gods in the afterlife. With this in mind, I believe that the evidence suggests that one of Egypt's most iconic images – the Djed Pillar, may also be related to the bee. But before revealing how and why, it is necessary to review another Egyptian image of great renown – the Ankh.

Reflections on the Ankh

Little is known for certain about the enigmatic symbol of the Ankh; indeed the website "Answers.com" informs us that, "The original meaning of this Egyptian symbol is not known." Like so many evocative images, the Ankh has been attributed with a wide spectrum of origins, ranging from the knot of Isis, a woman's womb, the sunrise, a penis sheath, the royal cartouche, and a plethora of other New-Age inspired associations. Refreshingly, the Egyptologist Sir Alan Gardiner observed that the word for sandal strap resembled the word Ankh, and that the loop around the ankle of the sandal closely resembled the image of the Ankh.

For adherents of Occam's Razor – a theory named after the fourteenth century English philosopher, William of Ockham, that stipulates that the simplest explanation is likely to be the most correct – we will start with that assumption. Gardiner's interpretation resonates, as does a variation on the theme that suggests that the Ankh was a camel shoe. Both interpretations highlight the fact that objects central to everyday life were held sacred for the domestic, yet vital, service they provided.

Similarly, the Ankh – whose definitions include "The key to the Nile" - may represent an Anchor. The English translation of the two names is linguistically similar and their respective designs are visually striking; each is a cross with a loop at the top.

I believe that any sea - or river - faring society would be indebted to the service that an anchor provides. And a Pharaoh, who is often portrayed with two ankhs - one in each hand - may have symbolically been grounding himself both in this life, and the next. And first-century saints in Rome had Ankh-like anchors carved on their tombs, while the image also appears frequently in Roman catacombs. Could the Ankh really have been an anchor? Occam's Razor seems to at least support the possibility.

Was the Sphinx a Bee Goddess?

Just as the Ankh may have been an anchor, or some other rudimentary object, the function of the Djed Pillar, arguably the most enigmatic of all Egyptian symbols, may also have its roots in domestic use. The Djed, like the bee, is strongly associated with the concept of stability. It's also associated with the god Osiris, prompting many scholars to believe that the Djed is "the backbone of Osiris." As previously discussed, Osiris is associated with bulls, regeneration and the bee. In fact, Djedu is the Egyptian word for Busiris, an ancient centre of his worship. Ultimately, this symbolism has prompted some to suggest that the Djed is actually the sacrum of a bull's spine – a common offering in ancient animal sacrifices. And in fact, sacrum in Latin is sacer, or "sacred," a translation of the Greek hieron, meaning sacred or strong bone.

Still others have associated the Djed with the Tree of Life, due to the myth that Osiris was imprisoned in a Tamarind tree, and the Djed's resemblance to a tree. This is understandable, as the Djed played a vital role in the "Renewal" or "Sed Festival," which was sometimes known as the "Festival of the Tail."

During this festival, the Pharaoh would run around an outdoor temple with a tail of a bull affixed to his regalia, stopping to shoot arrows in all cardinal directions in order to symbolically mark the boundaries of his kingdom.

With this in mind, interestingly, as a warrior Goddess, Neith is associated with archery – and arrows, as is Min, the pre-dynastic god whose titles included "Master of the Wild Bee." The Sed Festival, customarily held on the 30th anniversary of the king's reign, was Egypt-wide, although Luxor and Saqqara – sites of the Apis bull necropolis of regeneration - were arguably the most special.

The Sed Festival featured the Djed, which was ceremonially raised as a symbol of the potency and longevity of the pharaoh's rule. We have already noted how honey was believed to prolong life and was a vital ingredient in drinks used for magic and ritual. Not surprisingly then, the Djed is frequently depicted being presented to the Pharaoh's mouth in various reliefs and stele. And herein lays a clue to its possible function.

The raising of the Djed is depicted in many places and perhaps most notably at the religious centre of Abydos, where a secretive passion play took place in the presence of the King. Another centre known for its Djed raising rituals was Memphis – the domain of the god Ptah, who was known as "the Noble Djed." Memphis is also known to have had a sanctuary dedicated to the bee where noble women served as priestesses of the goddess Neith. Reliefs showing the raising of the Djed often depict the Djed with plumes, recalling the image of a bee-like antenna, as previously discussed.

So, we have learned that Egypt was the Land of the Bee, that the King was the Beekeeper and that honey was the Nectar of the Gods offered to the deities in the afterlife. In this context, might the Djed have simply been the instrument that administered honey – the "nectar of the gods," to the actual Gods? Might the Djed have been a form of honey dripper? Even the most cynical of observers could observe the similarity in design, function and context: each consisting of a pillar with a series of spherical circles on the top.

Suggesting that the Djed may have been a real or symbolic honey dripper does not deny that it, or for that matter the Ankh, did not also possess a deeper, more spiritual, and esoterically important meaning. It only suggests that its origins may very well have been mundane – even banal – and from that foundation sprang more sacred associations.

Lastly, before concluding our study of bee symbolism in ancient Egypt, we would be remiss if we did not explore the controversy surrounding the image of the Sphinx, for amazingly enough, it too may be related to the bee. The image depicted on the Sphinx has long been the source of speculation. A lioness is the most popular theory, and is supported by the legend of the gods Akeru; two lionesses who preside over the east / west axis, and hence the rising and setting sun. The gods are related to Horus, the god of the East; RA - the god of the midday sun; and Asar – the god of the night sun. The legend of two lion guardians has in recent times given rise to the belief that a second Sphinx may exists beneath the sands of the Giza Plateau, although this remains to be confirmed.

Others believe the image of the Sphinx portrays the jackal Anubis – or Anpu - and curiously, Anpu's skin is frequently represented by bees. Anubis was also known as the "Lord of the Hallowed Land," meaning necropolis, and his cult is thought to predate Osiris. And of course, we have the possibility that the 4th Dynasty King Khafre (2558 - 2532 BC) or his son and successor Radjedef, had the Sphinx re-carved in his own image, or obscured its identity – perhaps in an attempt to usurp an earlier matriarchal rule. After all, the Goddess Neith was worshiped more than most other Egyptian gods at the time of the King's reign.

Alternatively, as Khafre's pyramid most closely aligns with the Sphinx, and as he was the son of Khufu, whose pyramid was the grandest in all of Egypt, perhaps he re-carved the Sphinx in his own image in an attempt to "one-up" his father. Or, was it just the opposite? Might Khafre have re-carved the Sphinx in the very image of his father as a form of ancestor worship? Irrespective of these speculations, we may very well find a clue to the true identity of the Sphinx in its name.

The Sphinx was known by the ancient Egyptians as Hun nb, and most of us forget that it was the Greeks who named it Sphinx, a word believed to stem from the Greek verb σφιγγω, or sphiggo, meaning "to strangle." As this definition is somewhat difficult to grasp, we will briefly examine what other ancient cultures knew about the Sphinx, in the hope of gaining further insight.

For a start, the Sphinx was known as Abul-Hol in Arabic, which has been translated as "Father of Terror." The Sabians called it Hwl, which equates to the Egyptian Hu. Furthermore, the stele in front of the Sphinx refers to Hor-em-Akhet-Khepri-Re-Atum and Atum-Hore-Akhet, with Thutmosis being described as the Protector of the Horakhti. Egyptologists have often translated Hor-em-Akhet and Horakhti as Horus of the Two Horizons, which harkens back to the two guardian gods Akeru. In other words, these are the names of the Sphinx in the language of those whose monuments shared the plateau or who visited the site in antiquity. But has that helped us understand the true identity of the Sphinx? Just possibly the answer involves another culture altogether – that of the Minoans, the Bronze Age culture that flourished between 2700 and 1450 BC and originated on the island of Crete.

The Minoans existed in the same time and in some instances, in the same place as the ancient Egyptians and were experts in beekeeping, a craft they later imparted to the Greeks. And again, it was the Greeks who named the rock-hewn statue "Sphinx" in the first place. So how does all this relate to the bee? Quite simply, the Minoan word for Bee was sphex… (Hilda Ransome, *The Sacred Bee* P64, 1937).

So what can we conclude from this revelation? The civilization that educated the Greeks in the craft of beekeeping used the word "sphex" to describe the bee – and the Greeks named the goddess-like rock statue "Sphinx." Entertaining the scenario for a moment, does this mean that the Pharaoh Khafre re-shaped the Sphinx with the intention of concealing its Mother Goddess-influenced origins? Could the Fourth Dynasty have involved an attempt to suppress the cult of the Mother Goddess and conceal the importance of the Goddess Neith – the goddess who existed before the other gods? Was the Sphinx already present when Menes first established Kingship and was it known that the Sphinx represented the bee, hence the Pharaoh's title, Beekeeper?

The Online Etymology Dictionary states that the definition of "Sphinx" includes: "Monster, having a lion's (winged) body and a woman's head." And "Sphex" in ancient and modern Greek refers to Wasps – similar to Bees. While further etymological work beckons, the implication that the Sphinx might in some way, shape, or form, represent a bee goddess remains highly intriguing, especially given the fact that legends of lions and bees and winged sphinxes are quite common in the ancient world.

The Sacred Bee Around the World

The veneration of the sacred bee was central to Egyptian life, having evolved from its initial and largely domestic contribution to agricultural sustenance. The tradition was inherited from their ancestors - most notably the Sumerians – and integrated into Egyptian society in such a discernible way that it was readily adopted by later societies, including the United States of America.

Greek mythology depicted bees on the statues of their most important gods and goddesses, and developed the honored position of female bee shamans, called Melissa's. Mayan culture venerated the bee and depicted gods in its image in their most sacred temples. The early Catholic Church adopted the bee as a symbol of the Pope's authority; evidence of which can still be seen in Vatican City today. Political movements, such as Communism, drew from the altruistic behavior exhibited in a beehive, as a blueprint for their ideologies, while rulers such as Napoleon followed the tradition of their ancestors; in this instance, the long-haired Kings of France known as the Merovingian's - believed by some to represent the bloodline of Christ - whose famous King Childeric was discovered buried with 300 bees made of solid gold. Not only did Napoleon ensure that the symbol of the bee was infused in the decor and style of the royal court, and greater society, he adopted "The Bee" as his nickname as well.

French Freemasonry soon spread to the United States of America, aided by early American forefathers such as Thomas Jefferson, who wrote passionately about the importance of bees, while others such as President George Washington, featured the beehive on his Masonic apron. In no uncertain terms, early American society borrowed many of its philosophical principals from Freemasonry, which had incorporated bee symbolism and themes into its rituals, and established its government on the orderly, stable and "one for all" behavior exhibited in a beehive, like societies before them had done for thousand of years.

In fact, not only was the entire Western Region of the United States originally named after the bee (Deseret) but America's most iconic statue – Washington's Monument – pays homage to the sacred creature in an astonishing way; it contains an inscription that recalls the importance of bees throughout history, it states: "Holiness to the Lord Deseret," meaning "Holiness to the Lord, the

Honeybee." The existence of this peculiar dedication, let alone its meaning, has largely been forgotten – or at least ignored - but those with eyes to see will know that it hails from a golden age in Egyptian history when the veneration of the sacred bee was embraced by all facets of life.

# # #

Andrew Gough is an enthusiast of a variety of esoteric subjects, from the mystery of Rennes-le-Château to the lost esoteric tradition of the Sacred Bee and the hidden identity of the Egyptian Pharaoh Khufu. He has traveled the ancient world extensively and has written for journals and publications of all sorts, including a de-coding of *The Da Vinci Code*, in Simon Cox's best-selling book, *The Dan Brown Companion* (Mainstream 2006).

Andrew has a passion for Egypt, and has participated in the Eastern Desert Survey, an initiative to record and catalogue pre-dynastic rock art. Until its termination, Andrew was Director of the Institute of Interdisciplinary Sciences, and is currently Chairman of the longest running Rennes-le-Château research society, The Rennes Group. He is a regular guest - and presenter - on the syndicated esoteric television talk show, *Gardiner's World*, and his website, www.andrewgough.com includes a popular discussion forum featuring research on a variety of mysteries. Andrew moved from Chicago to England in 1996 and currently works and lives in London.

Portals to the Past: A Contemporary Experience of Ancient Monumental Culture

By Jasmine Gould, Archaeologist

As an archaeologist, much of one's time is spent kneeling in the soft dark earth, often in the rain, wondering exactly why repeatedly grazing one's knuckles to pursue knowledge from our ancestors can help us connect with our past, when surely all we will discover (if we are lucky) are shards of pottery, some broken stone tools or the remains of an archaic structure. As a Pagan who grew up in the countryside and spent a childhood under the leafy canopies of our forest home, running across breeze stroked hillsides of the Scottish Borders, punctuated by weathered standing stones and the knowledge that under my bare feet Romans used to play marbles by the side of their new and precise road, I can't help feeling a pre-destined motivation for the mystical connection I feel to the landscapes' history and its ritual uses.

How can we ever get a real sense of how ancient cultures lived, how they thought, what their hopes and fears were from a few tiny fragments? We are so embedded in our post-industrialist paradigm that we've eschewed our connection to the planet itself in favour of the machines we've constructed upon it and with that comes a loss of our ability to experience our environment, forgotten how it is, as a living being, to interact with our environment authentically, in ways our archaic predecessors did.

Perhaps, then we should look up and out at those first monumental attempts to engage with terra firma – those stoic stones, the megaliths; punctuating our lands, cryptic, alluring and to most people inaccessible in terms of how our ancestors viewed them.

What we require is an approach to experiential and sensual interactions with those purposefully integrated archaic, physical features in the landscape, to engage meaningfully with our landscapes, natural and fabricated. The inspiration for this "lived experience" perspective was inspired by three books: Chris Tilley's *The Materiality of Stone: Explorations in landscape Phenomenology,* and *Symbolic Landscapes,* by Paul Deveraux. The third work is Ronald Hutton's *Pagan Religions of the British Isles: Nature and Legacy.* This book I recommend as a "third way" and intermediary work, archaeological and academic in premise, but structured for lay reading, it is extremely accessible. Here, he attempts to reconcile the academic and the new-age views of prehistoric sites as something spiritual and worth understanding as a conduit through which we can access the past.

The first two works contrast starkly and are what one can consider the academic and the popular viewpoints, on how we, as modern humans, experience and relate to the natural environment and its archaic megalithic enhancements by ancient peoples.

Let us first examine the current academic perspective favoured by Tilley. One must keep in mind that Tilley is an anthropologist and as such, endeavours to utilise a post-modernist, Interpretive approach. So this is as much about how something "seems to us" as well as "what is really there." Tilley applies a metaphysical, philosophical mode of thinking, which enables us to relate what is "really there" with "what appears to us" to be there.

His acknowledgment of Merleau-Ponty illustrates that we may require skills and tools from other disciplines to aid us in understanding and interpreting what we are experiencing. Tilley uses Merleau-Ponty's definition concurrent with his own motivations in philosophically explaining how we perceive the landscape and I would like to relate this to how we perceive megalithic remnants of past peoples. According to Merleau-Ponty, Phenomenology "... is a philosophy for which the world is always 'already there' before reflection begins - as an inalienable presence; and all its efforts are concentrated upon re-achieving a direct and primitive contact with the world, and endowing that contact with a philosophical status… It also offers an account of space, time and the world as we 'live' in them." (1962: vii, in Tilley 2005: 1)

I will use East Aquhorthies circle in Aberdeenshire and the archetypal site of Stonehenge. What I want you to do now, is to think about a standing stone,

stone circle or megalithic environment you may have visited, read about or even just wish you could visit. Now try to become aware of how this mental recapturing of time and place makes you feel. What aspects of the place do you recall? This should begin to illustrate what Tilley and Merleau-Ponty are describing when they attempt to relate what we physically experience with how it is sensually experienced. What you are doing when you concentrate upon a memory or thought is entering into a self-invoked, light trance-state.

Our physical body is the primary mode of experience: we see, touch; even smell, hear or taste the world around us – the five Aristotelian senses give us a basic interaction with our landscape.

But what about other senses, say, of time and place? Sense of wonder or confusion? Sense of scale and proportion? Sense of history, or something mystical. Is the surface of the monolith smooth or rough beneath your touch? Perhaps you even hear the colors, or see the sounds. This synaesthetical awareness collects together a multitude of abstract sensual experiences to form a "real lived" awareness of your surroundings. Even if two people are imagining Stonehenge, they will both be experiencing different things, different aspects; maybe one is imagining the circle in daylight, surrounded by other visitors, another may be picturing the place at sunset, the rays of light streaming through the gaps in the darkened stones. If you are picturing the ancient site, are you outside the circle, or inside? Are the stones to your right or left, in front or behind you?

This is what Tilley is attempting to address – one's meta-physical relation to the physicality of what you are actually experiencing. He calls this an "ontological ground for the study of things" (2005:29).

I want you to think about this as you recall, and think about what the site you are recalling means to you in terms of what you experienced. It is with this in mind I wish you to indulge me a moment while I recount my phenomenological experience. It is this sense of "lived experience" of the world that, when I visited East Aquhorthies last year, made me feel and remember the various things I do. In that sense, my recall of the stones as warmed by the evening sunshine, the fragrance of meadowsweet in the air and the sense of camaraderie and fellowship with my dig buddies became part and parcel of how I personally experienced the stone circle. In our reveries, daydreams or concentrated thought upon these megaliths, we are invoking a trance state

– through which we connect to the unconscious – and begin to enable us to experience these places as would have been experienced by those who first constructed them. We may never know exactly why the circles were formed, or why solitary stones are placed where they are, but we can begin to perceive of how they would have been interacted with physically and meta-physically.

Tilley says "places gather together persons, memories, structures, histories, myths and symbols. Mental and material, symbolic and practical, wild and domestic, they constitute landscapes, collections of space-bounded structures and meanings" (2005:25). We might bring to mind Levi-Strauss' Structuralist concept of binary oppositions. Levi-Strauss also noted that not only do we work in myths, but myths work in us. (1978)

I sat inside the circle, with my back against a stone. I could see the far hill tops, the woods and fields. I felt timeless and embedded in the here-and-now all at the same time. The song of the lark and the hum of the bees were the same as they would have been five thousand years ago. The mead I had drunk formed the "soft-focus" pictures I hold in my memory. The honeyed taste of the mead became interwoven with my memory of the stones, so that as I recall East Aquhorthies, the honey becomes part of the stone – I synaesthetically taste the stone.

My "situatedness" in my worldview made me experience this place as mystical. The recumbent stone over which the Midsummer sun would have risen, cradled between the uprights physically remains just as those contemporary peoples would have seen it. Bennachie, the hill from which the massive red granite blocks came, would still have been situated in the landscape where it looms today. I was physically experiencing the land as a ritual landscape, just as the ancestors had. Places such as these are inherently transformative – inside the circle is another world, it is the doorway to the intangible world of spiritual awareness – I stood upon the threshold of prehistory.

This brings me to the second and Popularist perspective: the Mythologised Landscape. Here we must remind ourselves of Merleau-Ponty's notion that phenomenological perspectives concentrate "upon re-achieving a direct and primitive contact with the world" (ibid). Deveraux's work in the fields of sacred geography attempt to reconcile the ancient way of thinking and experiencing landscape with the current wide spread beliefs about sites, like Stonehenge, as part of a mythological landscape.

The popular view is of prehistoric use of the monument as a centre of sun worship. This is a ritual that is re-enacted and enjoyed by people every year at the summer solstice. Many believe the druids built and used the site as a solar ritual centre. However, anthropologist Lionel Sims believes they may have used Stonehenge as a ritual centre, not only at Midsummer, but at Midwinter. Simms believes that sunset was of paramount importance perhaps the moon was also worshipped there on the longest night – a lunistice: the absolute antithesis of the popular view. What "actually" occurred there is rather different to what is perceived as happening there...

Stonehenge, Ronald Hutton believes, is a ritual centre; this is a site that joins earth and sky, people and the cosmos, the mundane and the spiritual. The popular contemporary belief holds this to be true and has mythologized Stonehenge to be one of ritual, of druidic sun-worship. These views are about empowering the individual, being aware of the otherwise subconscious, making a connection with the past - remember Merleau-Ponty's notion that this is about making a connection through something "direct and primitive" though anthropologically, we might prefer to call it pre-logical or pre-scientific.

What we are engaging in here is essentially non-linear, magical thinking. And where magical thought is concerned, scientific lines of enquiry are of little or no use. We cannot rationalise something that defies logic, though we can seek to explain it.

Here I wish to briefly return to altered states of consciousness, which are integral to ritual and one could apply this alteration of mind/brain state to phenomenological thought as much as to how these sited were originally perceived. Altered States of Consciousness (ASC's) have been defined as any mental state recognized by the individual as different from his or her normal waking consciousness.

A state of consciousness that differs significantly from baseline or normal consciousness often identified with a brain state that differs significantly from the brain state at baseline or normal consciousness. (www.altered-states.net)

Deveraux cites Carl Jung who wrote that "myth-forming structural elements must be present in the unconscious psyche," this is what is occurring with this constructed, popular contemporary view of megaliths. By forming a mythologized landscape, people are attempting a phenomenological connection with the past by transforming their thoughts – as you recall your experiences in your megalithic sites – you are altering your state of consciousness. This is the other-worldly quality megalithic sites are designed to evoke. By altering your state of consciousness, you can access your "unconscious psyche," making a connection with the ancestors, times past and their legacy. You are experiencing something that transcends time and space and that is what phenomenological perspectives are attempting to achieve – it matter not what is actually there, in a sense – but what seems to be there to you. You are being transformed by your experience.

That is not to say that we cannot have absolute knowledge about the past, but what we are concerned with here is not only what the megaliths are "really, actually" like – but how they seem to each and every one of us individually. It is the phenomenology of landscape and of megaliths that allow us to make connections across the centuries and millennia – what we must endeavour to do is to be aware of this, be mindful, and thus, we can experience megaliths like Stonehenge or East Aquhorthies the way our ancestors did. When I remember the East Aquhorthies, I indelibly imprinted, not only the roughness of the stone against my back through my soil-stained dig T-shirt, or the waft of greening meadowsweet from the hedgerows, but the passing of eons, the forces of the elements and the touch of countless hands. I felt the wind and rain of five thousand years, I sensed the passing of suns and moons overhead and realized nothing had changed.

Except perhaps our impressions of what the landscape means to us. We all, each one of us, have an inner landscape where the rains wash the soft stones and the wind scours the hard.

Okay, so I may romanticize, but isn't that what making a connection with something wonderful does to us? Next time you visit a monumental site perhaps you can experience it through a new perspective. You can pass through the portal and into the past.

Bibliography and References

Deveraux, P (1995) *Symbolic Landscapes. The Dreamtime Earth and Avebury's Open Secrets.* Glastonbury, Gothic Image Pubs.

Hutton, R (1991) *The Pagan Religions of the British Isles: Their Nature and Legacy.* Oxford: Blackwell

Levi-Strauss, C (1966) *The Savage Mind.* London: Weidenfield and Nicholson

Merleau-Ponty, M (1962) *Phenomenology of Perception.* London: Routledge

Merleau-Ponty, M (1968) *The Visible and the Invisible.* Evanston IL, Northwestern University press

Pennick, N (1989) *Practical Magic in the Northern Tradition:* Aquarian Press

Scarre, C (2002) *Monuments and Landscape in Atlantic Europe: Perception and Society During the Neolithic and Early Bronze Age.* London: Routledge

Sims, L (2006) *The "Solarization" of the Moon: Manipulated Knowledge at Stonehenge.* Available at www.radicalanthropologygroup.org/pub_sims_solar_moon.pdf

Tilley, C. (2005) *The Materiality of Stone: Explorations in Landscape Phenomenology: 1.* New York, Berg

Web: www.altered-states.net

#

Jasmine Bonning gained her MA in Archaeology & Social Anthropology from the University of Edinburgh. In a considered attempt to reconnect with the authentic world view of our ancestors, she has chosen to explore the use of color in archaic ritual and ancient magical practice, while she is also interested in European megalithic culture and in the phenomenology of the prehistoric mind. She writes extensively on these subjects, and in addition to her specialised studies in the fields of anthropology and ethnography, she works on site, on archaeological excavations in Scotland and the Western Isles, concentrating on the remote Palaeolithic and the more recent Bronze and Iron Age eras, in an endeavour to bring to light meaningful information about the cultural practises of our ancestors. She was involved in discovering Scotland's only Iron Age cobbled road and helped bring the largest "royal" roundhouse in Scotland to light. Jasmine is director of Archaeosophia, a company that specializes in archaeological and ethnographic research and writing for the creative media industry; in this capacity, she has recently been invited to produce a major media project aimed at completely revolutionizing the way we view one of the world's most famous ancient monuments. www.archaeosophia.co.uk

The Ancient Code

By Dan Green

I can easily believe that there was an Ancient Code, and still is, if we but know where to look for it. It may well be the one and the same as referred to as "The Green Language" of Fulcanelli, "The language of the Birds" and now more recently termed the "Rabbit Language" of the Knights Templar ... presumably as it has gone underground and that you have to burrow for it! I personally came across it as the lost Mother Tongue, a means whereupon all languages of the many thousands of the world's residents are placed into a cosmopolitan melting pot, into a common matrix producing a flawless Esperanto capable of providing accurate and endless information deduced from any one word, a word that will without fail metamorphose, constantly changing, never running dry, on and on to link the vastness of all known alphabets and their words, as first the ancient Buddhism taught that everything is linked to everything, and now modern physics are saying the same. If everything is linked to everything, then so too must all language be. The "paper chase" of the word is as infinite as the mathematical figure Pi.

The Ancient Code was/is a code of Conduct, and that conduct is related in obedience to Nature. The word "code," from French, concerns codex – more correctly "Code X" – the X-factor of the algebraic first unknown quantity, a codex being a manuscript volume, from "codicis" meaning "trunk of a tree," (the Tree of Life) set of tablets, a book. I have learned that Language comes from all natural sound and phenomena. This is why everything can talk to us, we can read the unwritten, hear conversations in the wind – everything has its own speak. The onomatopoeia of a whispering or babbling brook the howling gale of a banshee-like wind that gives rise to ghost stories, the pitter-patter of the earliest drops of the precipitous rainfall, the buzz of the busy honey gathering bee, the "bless you!" and "atchoo!" of the forceful sneeze, the booming snore of the person deep in sleep. We have lost most of our ability to communicate with a talkative Nature, replacing it with the noise pollution of our modern societies in its myriad forms of road traffic, aircraft, helicopters, noisy neighbors, pubs and clubs, trains and industrial activities, road works, building sites, demolition, machines and telephones at work, and the commercial noise of the shopping centers. The cumulative strain on our nervous systems has now taken its toll and we are a population of stress, many faltering and falling into the abyss of depression and related mental ill health. Many are the invisible rays that pass through our buildings from radio, microwave, infrared rays and magnetic fields – if we could see them all in one go we'd go insane. We invoke these modern angels and demons regularly into our living rooms at the press of a button, and have drowned out Nature's soft speak supplanted by the persuasive diction of commerce with the kerching of maniacal cash machines. Give me the *I Ching* anytime.

Sadly, the Age of Technology failed to live up to its promise of a Space Age for all. Back in 1968 I sat in the cinema watching the Kubrick epic *2001- a Space Odyssey,* not only trying to work those last twenty minutes out as a confused twelve year old, but thinking to myself, "Well, it's thirty-two years off but its bound to be worth the wait." Came the Millennium, no monorails in the sky or day trips to the moon, and still wobbly chimney pots up on rooftops. Only multi-billionaires like Richard Branson can afford to take their family beyond those fluffy white clouds. Abandoning nature to sell our soul for technology, sadly, we have missed the point and bypassed our unique connection with nature to venture dangerously deep within a materialistic society and in doing so have endangered our individual psyches. Multiply this by every culprit and we have the amalgamate global problems and kick back from nature that we have today. The climate will change and become more hostile but the planet will always adapt, but will or can we? Is it too late to rediscover the ancient code and re-evaluate our conduct, that conduct that has acted like conductivity transmitting and turning up the heat? And what of those of us who haven't been as guilty? Nature has often warned us, did She not do so in places as far apart as the Kogi tribe of Columbia high up their mountain they call "The heart of the world" and the earliest days of the Findhorn community. In 1990 the Kogi's felt they had to address the rest of the world – the snows had stopped falling there and their rivers were not so plentiful. If their mountain was ill then so was the world. In the early '70s funky Findhorn at Moray in Scotland had its own ambassador, no less than the god of Nature, Pan himself! Although I have no doubt that this rustic deity's communications were the neurological product of the collective unconscious and appropriate archetypes manifesting through its chosen and preferred, the messages contained within are no less valid. Archetypes are ever changing when it comes to announcing to the masses that the planet is in danger, and currently the "UFO" is working overtime from "abductions" to close encounters, its presence confidently predicted by Carl Gustav Jung as far back as 1947 when the critters first put in their enigmatic appearances. Not so much aliens as the many faceted psychic manifestations of our planet talking to us in a veiled visual language, from the thinking super-organism that this globe is. It makes me wonder, do we really own our own brains, or do we lease it much like how we may own our own television sets but have to pay a license for the privilege of broadcasts coming through it? Full marks to Blavatsky and her cosmic theosophical proclamations at her time introducing us to Devas and landscape angels, and to Lovelock for his timely Gaia theory and hypothesis. Yes, the planet is communicating to those who hear, and we best pay heed. How best? Respect for the Ancient Code of natural conduct ... it may be too late for prevention and for what we are to collectively face by way of the Is-to-Be, but singularly I feel it isn't too late for any individual. Our actions and thoughts are registered by the Mind that belongs to the planet and so we must be preparing for that raising consciousness that is going on all about us, resist it and we will be a casualty. Allow me to relate my own example. I have visited the Tor at Glastonbury, Somerset, numerous times since 1985. It is, without doubt, a powerful and natural energy grid. I have visited it all times of the day, all seasons and in all weathers. It is perhaps my most favorite place on earth. In 2005 I visited my old friend for the first time carrying a camera, my thinking aloud asking it if it was possible for me to record any aerial phenomenon that could occur at this energy point. If the earth be an actual planetary body, it will have its own acupuncture points and some have been duly recognized and celebrated. Any such phenomenon that can pick up on sensitive chemical film would correctly show us manifestations we would expect relating to a body from biological cells and plasma. Our brains would scramble such evidence to make it safely digestible to our understanding and so we would see, perhaps, the archetype of the UFO. That June when I reached two-thirds of the steep ascension of the Tor, I became unexpectedly filled with such a sudden panic that I was convinced I was going to have to head back down – not my style! Was the archetype of the god Pan, who is known to instill Pan-ic, awaiting my arrival and therefore I was feeling his presence? I eventually made it to the top and Michael's Tower although the apprehension never left me. I took some pix and, yes, some manifestations were "granted." Maybe I had to pay a forfeit for the pleasure? The following year when I found my feet climbing the famous hillock again, and at the exact same point, that overpowering feeling of trepidation returned, only this time even worse. Convinced again that I was going to head back down, I managed, as before, to somehow regain a modicum of composure to reach the summit still with that intense uneasiness. I took some more pix and a strange "x" shaped cross appeared in exactly the same position, to the right of the Tower, as it had the previous year! My last visit saw that horrific alarm wash over me again. This time, after convincing myself this was the year I was going to run away as the "attack" was worse than the previous two combined, when I did re-enact the unnerving climb to the summit, the irrational emotion thankfully subsided and I felt more akin to how I had always felt upon there on my many previous and untroubled visits.

Incidentally, no photographic manifestations to speak of that time.

So what had all that been about? I know that the Tor as an area that can "think and receive thoughts" had clearly been aware of my intentions and it appears it reciprocated. But something there was clearly different for me, and I have no doubt it had to do with the changes that are going on in the world, under the world and above it. It is so strident that none of us are exempt. But amidst the turmoil all ended well, and I feel that for those who are in attunement with and have their own connection with nature the outcome will ultimately be the same. As the old song warbles, "There may be trouble ahead..." it'll be a bumpy ride for sure but if we fasten our seat belt and hold onto our hat, and with heed to the Ancient Code, as respectful individuals I think we might just make it.

# # #

Dan Green is the author of *The Lincoln Da Vinci Code* and *The Lincoln Da Vinci Code and the Mystery of Rennes-le-Chateau* and is currently working on a DVD encapsulating the work. In 1977 he studied Kalachakra Vajrayana at the Karma Kagyu Samye-Ling Tibetan Centre and Monastery at Dumfriesshire, Scotland under the patronage of a Rinpoche Teacher, and has met HH the Dalai Lama. Having lived the first forty years of his life in the North

East of England, he was instrumental in the national adult comic "VIZ," has worked in local and national television and within the music business, creating surreal comedy characters for each. He has contributed articles for paranormal magazines and has appeared on television with his *Lincoln Cathedral Code*. He has a cult following on the internet where he contributes regular features for a variety of sites and for his YouTube videos. With an interest in neurology, Dan has a wife and son with high functioning Asperger's Syndrome and his academic limited edition book *Buddha and the Autist* on the subject of the puzzle of autism has been appraised by leading UK expert Prof. Simon Baron-Cohen at his Autism research Centre at Cambridge University, and world expert on savants, Darold Treffert at his research centre in Wisconsin.

Dan is a celebrated figure where he lives in the East Midland city of Lincoln.

Suns of God

By Dr. John Jay Harper

"The workings of the human body are an analogy
for the workings of the universe."

Leonardo da Vinci
(April 15, 1452 – May 2, 1519)

Based upon his book *Tranceformers: Shamans of the 21st Century*

ABSTRACT: The Great Pyramid at Giza contains the secret to the eternal cycle of life, death and rebirth in our cosmos; the so-called Riddle of the Sphinx. This article reveals that formula of reincarnation within the star clusters of the Orion Nebula. In fact, it is the same story of creation embodied in the design of crop circles, sacred site stone megaliths, and the Zodiac that speaks to our origins and destiny as a star-seeding civilization. Indeed, there is an ancient yet modern truth bar-coded into our genes: The human soul is a magnetic monopole but as the Egyptians realized our soul splits into twins, the Ka and Ba. These two bipolar entities however must be restored to integrity, wholeness, here and now in order to open the star gates to our physical immortality. This is the meaning to what Jesus commanded in the *Gospel of Thomas*: "Make the two, one again!" He was speaking to the science of soul: Kabalah. The focus of the mystery school initiations was to "cross oneself" by aligning the seven major chakras with the subtle energy grid matrix of the Earth, Sun and Galaxy: The Cross of Christ. This then is the meaning to the

Second Coming of the Suns of God: Jesus, Osiris, Quetzalcoatl, and many other superstars in era-2012.

Introduction

Once upon a time in the outskirts of the Milky Way Galaxy, creatures calling themselves homo sapiens, a Latin word meaning "wise or knowing man" lived in one of its smaller solar systems on a very small planet they nicknamed "dirt" or Earth.

Ironically, they were not wise, knowing—or unique.

They had simply forgotten their birth origins and destiny as celestial beings of the Orion Nebula, the birthplace of stars, the Suns of God on Earth.

So over the course of centuries, as they gazed into the night sky sitting around campfires yearning for clues, a sign from on high, they told each other creation stories, myths, and performed acts, rituals, to explain why they were in this predicament.

Some religionists said they sinned against a god, in one form or another, a being that had returned to the sky. That they were now quarantined on Earth until a "savior," in one form or another, returned as promised at the end-of-time.

Others of these so-called "wise men" known as scientists taught humans were accidents of a blind and dumb gene-generating universe; freaks of nature, that gods and saviors did not even exist.

But then these myths and rituals, especially the ancient symbols used in astrology began to make sense, add-up, with the modern observations of astronomy. One of these homo sapiens named Carl Sagan even mused: "Some 25 million years ago, a Galactic survey ship on a routine visit to the third planet of a relatively common G dwarf star, our Sun, may have noted an interesting and promising evolutionary development: Proconsul, the ancestor of homo sapiens, or modern man."

Archaeologist, historian, and mythologist also known as D.M. Murdock, conclusively documents that major world religions are in fact founded upon an astrotheology: the story of stars as gods sent down from heaven to earth to save men from ignorance.

The larger realization based upon the overwhelming evidence suggests these humans represented the gods as action heroes on the ground to the people as she catalogues in her book *Suns of God: Krishna, Buddha, and Christ Unveiled*. Of course, we have Jesus himself saying: "I have said, you are gods; and all of you are children of the most High."

Nonetheless, once we saw the creation story focused through the lens of Galileo and later Hubble and Herschel telescopes, the lights came on to full-star power again across the entire spectrum of science and religion theories of origins.

And a whole new way of seeing ourselves not as freaks of nature but as a planned family of genetically engineered, star seeded, celestial beings emerged. Clearly, the occult, or hidden, records collected by esoteric societies were beginning to pay rich dividends too with respect to our relationship to stars.

One of these pioneers, Alice Bailey, reported: "In the secret of the Sun Sirius are hidden the facts of our cosmic evolution, and incidentally, therefore, of our solar system. The Sirius System is always beaming helpful rays to the poor people of Earth who wallow in appalling ignorance, violence, and oppression."

Suddenly the musings of mystics, shamans, and prophets of every culture made more sense, fit a pattern mirrored by stone structures at sacred sites worldwide; in particular Asia, Egypt, Mexico, England as well as the Hopi Nation in North America and Inca Empire in South America.

Egyptologist Wallis Budge, and others, linked the stars in Sirius, Orion, and Pleiades with emitting spiritual rays of light that "vivify gods, men, cattle, and creeping things … out of the seed of the soul." Budge even declared, "The mention of Orion and Sothis (Sirius) is interesting, for it shows that at one time the Egyptians believed that these stars were the homes of departed souls."

This rediscovered truth is straight-forward: We humans were designed to operate on a cosmic larger-than-life scale, as a "superman" mystics called Adam

Kadmon, and artist Leonardo Da Vinci portrayed as perfection personified in The Vitruvian Man. That is, our human body was the mathematical mirror-image of the Phi ratio Fibonacci series spiral, the golden mean of the Cosmos.

Overall, we see our self-image in a new light as that of a "superstar," the Sun of God, in fact, what theologian Matthew Fox calls The Cosmic Christ.

Plato was very clear in his treatise, *Timaeus*, that God made "souls in equal number with the stars and distributed them, each soul to its several star, and he who should live well for his due span of time should journey back to the habitation of his consort star."

"Consciousness is King," proclaimed philosopher of Rome, Plotinus, in the 3rd century A.D.

This then is true hidden knowledge: Stars are conscious beings of light and co-create planets for the development of infinite Christs-in-potential!

Gregory Sams, co-founder of the Harmony/Whole Earth Foods outlets in the United Kingdom, chaos theory expert, and now best-selling author of *Sun of God: Discover the Self-Organizing Force that Underlies Everything* has it spot on: "This is the greatest cover-up in history!"

In other words, human beings are created to live eternally as physical beings made of sunlight. We are Children of the Sun, and the Sun behind the Sun, the Mother Star Clusters in the Orion Nebula of our Milky Way Galaxy.

The Orion Nebula is the birthplace of our Sun's solar system and its life cycle known as World Sun Ages. The Maya, for example, saw the rebirth of Earth as beginning the Fifth Sun Age on December 22, 2012.

Ancients saw how species are seeded and mutated by starbursts, supernova explosions, solar flares, and Coronal Mass Ejections, or CMEs, as well as advanced civilizations. They saw cross-breeding between gods and men potentially helped evolve new cosmic creatures in an infinite loop of creation, destruction, and recreation: the life, death, and rebirth cycle of Suns of God.

This was hinted at in the *Holy Bible* that such was the case as in Genesis 6:4: "There were giants in the earth in those days; and also after that, when the sons of God came in unto the daughters of men, and they bare children to them, the same became mighty men which were of old, men of renown."

Now scientists agree: we are Star Children:

"In a very real sense," says University of Illinois astrophysicist Larry Smarr, "we are the grandchildren of supernovas."

Harvard professor of astronomy, Robert Kirshner, says, "Generations of supernovas created the elements we take for granted—the oxygen we breathe, the calcium in our bones, and the iron in your blood are products of the stars."

Fascinatingly enough, these sacred site ruins that we have turned into tourist traps can now become star map repositories of invaluable star seed information to reclaim our origins and destiny according to many scholars of them today.

And as we dug deeper into the forensic evidence of sacred sites, examined the blood, bone, and stones, so to speak; we decoded the meaning of the 12 signs of the times: the houses, mansions, or constellations the Greeks named Zodiac, or Circle of Animals. Again, it was Jesus who said: "In my Father's house are many mansions, I go and prepare a place for you."

So Zodiac signs were used to assign specific energy signatures to stars in the night sky with stones carefully crafted on the ground to create a mirror image of their consciousness traits. This maps the 12 characteristics of constellations. Our own star's life cycle through time and eternity in what we know now as a 26,000 year precession of the equinox of The Great Year.

Naturopathic health practitioner Amalia Camateros, proclaimed in her book *Spirit of the Stones: A Revival of Earth Wisdom*, based upon insights into the Anasazi of the American Southwest: "This knowledge was stored in the rocks as living libraries and kept safe within until a future time."

Stones are in effect sponges: they absorb and store consciousness that is carried by 12-rays of sunlight. Our human brain has 12 cranial nerves and earth 12 major tectonic plates to process light energy through them too. Needless to say, 12 is a key number to life, death, and rebirth as it defines, partitions, or sectors space itself into 12 signs of the Zodiac.

Perhaps, that is the greatest insight of so-called pagan cultures; they saw space is alive, conscious, with the ebb and flow of subtle solar radiation energy pulsations permeating everything forever. There isn't anything new under the Sun other than a cosmic recycling program of celestial beings through a mixing and matching of star systems within galaxies.

Pyramids are The Word of God Written in Stars and Stone

Distinguished writer Adrian Gilbert, stated this much in his book *2012: Mayan Year of Destiny*: "By building a gigantic scale model of Heaven on Earth, they were establishing a psychic link to the stars of Orion/Osiris. Then, by carrying out certain funerary rituals, such as the 'Opening of the Mouth' and 'Weighing of the Heart,' within the confines of the pyramids, they could assist the pharaoh's soul in its journey to the land of Osiris: the stars of Orion."

Alan F. Alford of Walsall, England declares: "Ancient sages believed that the future destiny of mankind lay in a return to the Source, i.e. to God and Heaven. The death of the body, they said, did not mark an end but rather a critical mid-point in the human existence. Those who had the secret knowledge could retrace the path to the Heavenly Source and enter the gates to the lost paradise. The knowing soul would then unite with its primeval body-double and materialize in a remarkably Earth-like world."

Ultimately we have rediscovered the secrets to reincarnation that were embedded in The Great Pyramid stones at Giza and the tombs in the Valley of the Kings. They and other related sacred site structures all seek to help us recapture our roots in the stars and point us back home to our Twin Earth in the "star nursery" of the Orion Nebula.

What we've learned is pyramids were not burial tombs, but time bombs! They speak to the end-time of the Earth's Shift on its polar axis realigning us with our home among the stars in the 21st Century now.

Indeed, our "god fathers" or Higher Selves are alive in a twin binary star earth-like system of planets defined by star clusters in the vicinity of the Orion, Sirius, and Pleiades constellations.

Robert Temple, the highly-acclaimed investigator of the Dogon tribe cultural myths in Africa, and also a member of the Royal Astronomical Society in England stated forthrightly in his classic text *The Sirius Mystery: New Scientific Evidence of Alien Contact 5,000 Years Ago*:

"Sirius was, astronomically, the foundation of the entire Egyptian religious system. Its celestial movements determined the Egyptian Calendar, which is even known as the Sothic Calendar."

Sirius, the Dog Star, is the prime candidate for our Sun's binary, double, or twin star system.

This insight is shared by archaeo-astronomer Walter Cruttenden, the Executive Director of the Binary Research Institute in Southern California in his book titled *Lost Star of Myth and Time* and DVD *The Great Year*.

The Orion Revelation

First and foremost, we look to the Orion Nebula to get oriented in the night sky, as did all the wayfarers on the ground that created the major sacred sites worldwide we have rediscovered.

Indeed NASA has named its new fleet of spacecraft replacing the space shuttle series in 2010, Orion. "Many of its stars have been used for navigation and guided explorers to new worlds for centuries," says Orion project manager Skip Hatfield.

Orion, "The Hunter" in Greek mythology, is one of the largest constellations of star clusters visible everywhere from Earth. It straddles the celestial equator and is a navigational beacon, a lighthouse, to ships at sea and outer space.

This much we know: Orion, Sirius, and Pleiades are calling us to look up again, but pay attention to the Pyramid Text messages typed in stone on the ground at the Giza plateau outside of Cairo.

Many scholars have blazed a trail for us to follow back home to these stars, in particular Graham Hancock, author of *Fingerprints of the Gods*, and *Heaven's Mirror*. Also Adrian Gilbert and Robert Bauval, the sojourners tracking Orion's "three belt stars" in the landmark book *The Orion Mystery*.

And Zechariah Sitchin in *The Earth Chronicles Handbook*. He is an authority on the ancient Sumerian language that predates writing to 3500 B.C. with manuscript fragments speaking to the existence and significance of a Planet "X" that may be in a cycle of eternal return, or binary orbit with Earth.

In his text *The 12th Planet* published in 1976, Sitchin wrote with respect to extraterrestrial genetic engineering and the human race: "Man is the product of evolution; but modern Man, Homo sapiens, is the product of the "gods."

Quite clearly we are witnessing a common theme: We are not alone and never have been but we have been lost in outer space that we could not see through with our third eye open. That is what all the mystics, prophets, and shamans have declared as the truth throughout the Dark Ages: We are blind and dumb to inner space now. Philosopher of religion Jeremy Naydler stated in *Temple of the Cosmos: The Ancient Egyptian Experience of the Sacred*: "In ancient times, by contrast, inner space was regarded as objective and as existing independently of the human psyche."

However, it was Egyptologist John Anthony West in his book *Serpent in The Sky: The High Wisdom of Ancient Egypt*, that solved the riddle of the Sphinx for me with his symbolic insights into the Temple of Man at Luxor.

For in its crumbling ruins, we find carefully crafted stones harmonically calibrated to the sacred geometry of stars and our subtle energy chakra system; and thus our bones and blood are tuned to music of the spheres by them to Orion Nebula.

West confirms that it is dualism, our split-vision between the unconscious and conscious minds that blinds and binds us: "Duality as the call to unchecked chaos and multiplicity is symbolized by the 'serpent fiend, Apop,' who devours the souls of the dead and thus denies them reunion with the source [or God]."

Thus we learn that the supreme purpose of pyramids was to open our mind's eye to starlight.

By example, I include the testimony of Greg Roach, an accomplished computer scientist who had a profound out-of-body vision triggered by a shaft of light in the "immaculate conception room" at the Temple of Seti I in Abydos, after viewing the Flower of Life images for the first time at the Osirion, an underground ceremonial chamber compared by some archaeologists to a Amerindian Kiva in the U.S. desert Southwest.

In his own words, Greg tells us:

"While on an Egyptian Tour visiting the Osirion in Abydos, I had a psyche-shattering experience in the form of a spontaneous, all-encompassing out-of-body vision. After a brief meditation in this Temple, I stood up into a shaft of light that came from an opening in the ceiling. This triggered the most massive change in consciousness I have ever experienced. My sense of the external world fell completely away and I stood in the presence of an ineffable, unexplainable, glory. To my inner eye it took the form of an infinitely recursive living electric fire. I was laughing and crying at the same time. My mind was filled to overflowing with the most remarkable awareness—a glimpse behind the veil and a true experience of the fundamental unity of life."

Of course, Osiris is the Egyptian Lord of love and the god of the afterlife in Orion and Sirius.

And I had a mountaintop experience with the starlight sparkling in Orion's Nebula in the winter of 2006.

While spending time in the old mining town of Republic, Washington, I happened to gaze up to the three belt stars in Orion. These stars were crystal-clear basking in that below-zero mile-high setting, and I immediately became mesmerized by them. I soon sensed a magnetic power flowing into my mind's third eye and was stunned by this simple rhyme playing in my head: "Twinkle, twinkle little star how I wonder what you are, like a diamond in the sky?"

Clearly, star alignment coordinates, if not creates, our states-of-consciousness on earth with respect to location and the receptive condition of our whole brain and central nervous system.

In fact, the major point I share in this article is credited to Professor Frederick Mills in Atlanta, Georgia, a man who dedicated 35 years of his life to decoding the Geometry of Divinity (or G.O.D.) symbols employed at sacred sites on Earth and Mars.

Fred had a spontaneous out-of-body experience while a graduate student at Texas Technological University that he attributes to his intense preoccupation with geometric symbols used in human communications theory. In many ways, it was the classic kundalini awakening of cosmic consciousness, yet he found himself looking back at Earth from the distance of our moon.

However, he observed the step-by-step sequence of events and knew that what was happening to him could be replicated for everyone who wanted it. Thus Mills launched into a lifetime search to find the golden mean, the dividing line between consciousness and unconsciousness, the key to trance phenomenon. For he knew that his technique can be used as the template for world peace: The experience of oneness with man, nature, and God.

Overall Mills' work bridges the gap between inner and outer space through opening the third eye with a unified field of cosmic consciousness as does the work of Roger Penrose in *The Emperor's New Mind* and Richard Hoagland in *The Monuments of Mars* respectively seek to do as well employing a fifth or hyper-dimensional model of physics.

Most recently, Robert and Olivia Temple captured this sacred wisdom of the golden section, the Phi ratio and Fibonacci series, in their textbook *The Sphinx Mystery: The Forgotten Origins of the Sanctuary of Anubis,* confirming what Mills and I have discussed for a decade. Specifically, the Logos, or the Word of God to the Christian community, is really a reference to this idea the Temple's and we share in common: "The Logos must be crucified to give the promise of eternal life by his resurrection."

Previously the Temple's had asked themselves: "But what is the meaning of the crucifixion? This is the remaining piece of the puzzle. The fact is that the crossbar of the cross represents the major of the upright of the cross divided in golden section, and by combining them … one was portraying the golden section by a symbol, a cross. Early drawings of crosses often had footbars. So the footbar is the minor, the crossbar is the major, and the upright is the sum of the two together. The minor and the major are in a ratio (logos). Crucified on the cross is the Logos himself, Christ."

In other words, Christ is the code of consciousness, the keyword, ratio, logos of the golden mean line segment sections of the Cross that Mills experienced consciously during his own crucifixion. His out-of-body "ego death" that is the feeling as one with Christ himself or Osiris to Egyptians or Quetzalcoatl to the Mesoamericans, and so forth. What Mills rediscovered is that we do not die at all because our limited sense of self becomes unlimited in that "Consciousness is King!"

From a science of soul perspective, the larger realization is that pyramids operate on this exact basic geometry set of principles unifying outer and inner space within one's third eye complex. And this is what the sacred sites were doing by aligning a mountain of stones with specific stars while performing initiating rituals during the seasonal crossings of the equinoxes and solstices: That is, they were crossing themselves in order to resurrect Cosmic Consciousness within them.

They were seeking to yoga or unite in a personal relationship with God again as it was in the Garden of Eden Golden Age.

In a real way, it is possible to build a communication device using earth stones much as we do in an electronic printed-circuit board in our laptop computer only with silicon chips as micro-stones yet configured in the same crystal-lattice matrix. Over and over again we see a Master Technology Plan in Pyramids: a satellite communications network linking sacred-stone sites to starlight solar-power sources overhead to self-empower them with information.

To be clear, the Egyptians were calibrating pyramids to very precise alignments with the Sirius star system, Orion's belt stars, the "Seven Sisters" of the Pleiades and the four fixed signs, Taurus, Leo, Scorpio, and Aquarius in the Zodiac. But especially was the Great Pyramid at Giza complex coordinated with the pole star Polaris in the 21st century—and we will soon see why: To alert us to the coming pole shift.

Therefore, this orientation of sky-to-ground is not a coincidence, a "trick of light and shadow," with respect to Orion in particular as well as Sirius.

Native American scholar of the Hopi, Gary A. David, has also mapped Orion to the high desert mesas in the State of Arizona, as he reveals in his books *The Orion Zone* and *Eye of the Phoenix*. In a recent article titled *Seeing Red: Will Betelgeuse Go Supernova in 2012?*, he speculates that "beetle juice," or Alpha Orionis, may have already in fact exploded with its light impacting our solar system and Earth only now.

Then Moria Timms described the effects of cosmic ray showers in her book *Beyond Prophecies and Predictions*: "In an instant, quicker than the eye could blink or the phosphene flare in the inner dimensions of the mind, the consciousness of the planet was encoded and imprinted. A superluminal transfer of extragalactic frequencies from deep space impregnated the Earth with the starseeds of neutrinos and radiation. Penetrating to the heart of the Earth's magnetic core, this jump-start of cosmic energy served to accelerate the vibrational frequency of the life force, preparing us for an unprecedented evolutionary leap."

And here is where we add that star-power fuel supply to the fire kindled in the pyramids, literally. For we now have the engineering data analysis report of Chris Dunn provided in his book titled *The Giza Power Plant*. Dunn found unmistakable residues in the King's Chamber of hydrogen gas combustion; that is to say, solar power.

But why we must ask; to do what for who and where?

I mean we find no residues of electric power pole lines used to light the cities in these regions; there are no airport runways, no interstate highways, or high-rise office buildings. There are no excavations unearthing an underlying asphalt jungle, in other words.

It is becoming obvious that our ancestors worshipped the stars for a very wise reason then: DNA tune-ups! They were fine-tuning their subtle energy "soul" body matrix, what Egyptians knew as the Ka and Ba twins, to the very same stars from which they came originally and therefore had a natural organic resonance.

Naturally, we are all made of stardust and we process sunlight through our solar-powered cells. We call that cycle of sunlight processing in plants "photosynthesis" and in fact that is why we eat the plants, and the animals that also eat those plants, to extract the trapped photons of light from them.

Of course, water, $H2O$, is the supreme source of life, and it too is made of the hydrogen plasma filaments cooked by suns and later condensed into green gaseous atmospheres by living planets.

So the evidence left behind by pyramids attests to a lifestyle that is organic, shamanic, and one in complete harmonic balance, or resonance, with the solar sunspot cycles of stars in the night sky.

Clearly these stone structures were solar collectors of sunlight, as well as celestial clocks, sunstone calendars calibrated to a 26,000 year cycle of the solstices, and equinoxes, with respect to the Zodiac.

In no uncertain terms, I'm saying sacred sites were designed in accordance with the star chart map of eternal life portrayed in the symbolisms of astrology and alchemy.

One example that speaks to this solar timing-pulse precision in Egypt is The Denderah Zodiac and we know the Mayan Calendar also had a similar purpose, forecasting the future on a galactic, solar, planetary, and personal scale of prediction.

So did the *I Ching, the Book of Changes,* in Asia.

It may also be the case these oracles, divining tools, were used to track the angle of tilt to our globe between World Sun Ages. Perhaps, a pole shift is a natural organic cycle, akin to how farmers rotate crops between seasons, leaving one section fallow and seeding the other section. Though this would place one land mass or continent underwater and bringing another up to dry land planting status again.

Author of *Pole Shift: Predictions and Prophecies of the Ultimate Disaster*, John White, has counseled as early as 1980: "Spiritual traditions warn that we shall reap what we sow. Psychic traditions offer an explanation of how and why this must be. The many 'crimes against nature' that people are perpetrating—over-population, environmental pollution, wasting of nonrenewable resources, nuclear testing—along with 'crimes against humanity' such as war, economic exploitation, the imposition of inhumane living conditions, religious persecution, political abridgement of human rights, intolerance and bigotry toward minorities, etc., are all pouring negative thought forms into the planet's energetic foundation. The result will be geophysical cataclysm: earth changes and a pole shift."

According to all indigenous cultures, the common denominator that triggers a pole shift is the Sun and its resonant relationship with the Suns behind Our

Sun, our Mother Stars within the Galactic Center.

Even human illness is triggered by radical changes in the Sunspot cycles, in particular, viral pandemics brought on by atmospheric changes in climate, that alter jet streams, creating extreme weather patterns and susceptibility to disease. In the final analysis, life is all about the feedback loop of cosmic consciousness that exists between Earth and Sun.

Sunspots shape the Sun's own atmosphere, its corona and solar wind; the short-wavelength solar radiation pulses from ultraviolet to X-ray. They regulate frequency of flares, coronal mass ejections, CMEs, and other solar eruptive phenomena, and modulate the flux of high-energy galactic cosmic rays entering our solar system from the Orion Nebula.

So, ready or not, space weather soon becomes earth weather.

Thus the purpose of Egyptian, and Mayan Sun-worship myths and rituals were scientific—not superstition—based upon a well-calculated survival strategy to routinely bring balance back to the North-South polar axis of The World Tree. In plain terms, pyramids are built to the Golden Mean Phi ratio spiral and the Fibonacci number series standards in order to align The Vitruvian Man with The Galactic Cross.

The Vitruvian Man

The Vitruvian Man is one of Leonardo da Vinci's signature creations that is dated to about 1487 A.D. The design is based upon the notes of Marcus Vitruvius Pollio; a Roman writer, architect, and engineer living 1500 years earlier. The image captures the human body as perfection in nature, the "measure of all things."

Da Vinci himself said, "The workings of the human body are an analogy for the workings of the universe."

We are speaking to the perfect man living in the perfect place called paradise: The Golden Age.

Mythologist Richard Heinberg reminds us in his book *Memories and Visions of Paradise: Exploring the Universal Myth of a Lost Golden Age*: "As human consciousness lost contact with its internal, heavenly source of power, technology emerged as a power substitute. Its first appearance was as sympathetic magic and as the invocation of spiritual beings to change Nature for human benefit. However, as human awareness became increasingly restricted to the material world, purely mechanical technologies appeared."

Indeed, sacred site stone megalith monument technologies are all constructed employing the Golden Mean Spiral. Jill Purce, author of *The Mystic Spiral* says, "The universal spherical Vortex is perhaps the most complete symbol by which we can map our cosmic journey."

My colleague, Fred Mills, in fact pointed out to me many years ago that The Vitruvian Man held a key insight into mapping the flow of cosmic consciousness through the double-helix spiral of our DNA macromolecule as well as the pyramids on Earth and Mars.

That is, the so-called Face on Mars and the pyramid complex on its Cydonia plateau mirror the Great Pyramid complex on the Giza plateau as the same geometry is encoded in these structures and The Vitruvian Man. You can overlay this man to the monument; those same angles, ratios, proportions, of the buildings are the human body in all its extraterrestrial glory in other words!

Clearly, there is a message in the fact that Cairo translates to an Egyptian word for Mars as well. It seems that once we connect-the-dots we witness that we are being invited to a family reunion of star-seeded children of the Suns of God.

Investigative mythologist William Henry wrote an article titled *Christ's Cosmic Wormhole*. In this third eye-opening treatise, he surveys the history of an instrument of space-travel known as the "djed column" or "Pillar of God."

He says that this is a forty-five foot tall golden-colored device located in "Temple complexes throughout the ancient world including Egypt and Solomon's Temple." Henry speculates the Pillar of God was used in a magical way to open up a vortex spiral, a tunnel into space-time realms throughout the universe.

Now a British academic writer in religious studies and classical philosophy,

Dr. Jeremy Naydler, author of T*emple of the Cosmos and Shaman Wisdom in the Pyramid Texts*, an expert in deciphering Egyptian glyphs and scripts from a mystical, shamanic perspective, says virtually the same thing: "The raising up of the djed column also symbolized the rebirth of the soul. For the Egyptians, the flow of life-giving forces into the world of nature was dependent upon the resurrection of Osiris 'on the other side' in the spiritual realm of the Dwat."

That spiritual realm is centered upon, as is the Great Pyramid, the belt stars of Orion Nebula.

Overall, we are looking at life-enhancing rituals that invoked the sensations of oneness, unity or cosmic consciousness here and now; the heavenly state-of-feeling connected testified to by all mystics, prophets, and shamans as the end-goal of creation: bringing Heaven to Earth.

Again, Richard Heinberg speaks to this desired state in *Memories and Visions of Paradise*:

"The Hopi legend of the First People says that they 'felt as one and understood one another without talking.' The original mind seems to have been a kind of living, pulsating web of telepathic interconnectedness, through the strands of which flowed a current of universal love."

In what the Egyptians called "Zep Tepi, the First Time in Orion," they could communicate telepathically with our mirror-image Twin Earth until the electromagnetic poles of the earth shifted, flipped the light switch off in our pineal gland, and we found ourselves in the Dark Ages—once again.

That is, our earth's ground-to-sky orientation to the Orion Nebula lost its calibration timing-signal, knocking us off the celestial equator centerline with it and out-of-touch with home base. We then suffered a catastrophic "fall from grace" and a failure to communicate with Mission Control!

We have been in the dark ever since unless a mystic, prophet, or shaman would share insights with us. This fact is illustrated convincingly by anthropologist Jeremy Narby in *The Cosmic Serpent: DNA and the Origins of Knowledge*.

That is why this multi-dimensional vision of reality was sought after in every culture using substitutes such as alcohol, tobacco, and potent mood-modifying as well as mind-altering drugs made of mushrooms, medicinal herbs such as ayahuasca tea vines, and marijuana plants.

Today this third eye open vision is triggered clinically by using hallucinogens containing DMT, Dimethyltriptamine to flood the pineal gland as has been well-documented by psychiatrist Rick Strassman in his text *DMT: The Spirit Molecule.*

This then is the spaceflight mission of The Vitruvian Man: To restore heaven on earth consciously in a renewed Garden of Eden. But as we know evolution is a brutal process and it will take our best and brightest efforts to survive the Polaris pole shift of the ages into Aquarius.

Indeed, Our Global Brain is being initiated into the mysteries of cosmic consciousness today as geo-scientist Gregg Braden conveyed in *Awakening to Zero-Point: The Collective Initiation* and Dr. Jose Arquelles alerted us in *The Mayan Factor: The Path Beyond Technology*: "The octahedral crystal—two tetrahedra joined together—is the radio-gyroscope holding the harmonic resonance of the Earth in its orbit. The crystal core catches or traps the galactic beams attracted to Earth by mutual resonance."

However, we remain blind and dumb as to the coming Earth Changes for the most part. Politicians and the mass media have our guts all twisted-up into knots over saving the economy when it's the ecology that will save our soul stupid!

We are the geometry, the ratio, Logos of the Word made flesh in the accelerating evolutionary spiral of a galactic-level mutation; biologically this is called a genetic "transposition burst" that is rewriting the non-coding or "junk" language of light codes within DNA.

This is a time of galactic genetic engineering, a cleansing cycle of enhancement as our sense of consciousness is reprogrammed by radiant bursts of star light energy in a new World Sun Age. Again, we call these magnetic pulses of information biophotons; they are signals from stars that communicate cell-to-cell throughout the entire life cycle of our light body and beyond to the zero-point field.

In other words, we are immortal celestial beings of light right now made of microscopic drops of DNA that are liquid-crystals of sunlight! But when we cannot see creation firsthand at the level of the biophotons through the lens of our third eye, we see only shadows of reality as portrayed symbolically by the images seen on the walls of Plato's Cave.

Hence, we see the severe clashes of cultures during these times of major earth changes in consciousness today especially. For we truthfully cannot see third-eye to eye because the language of the birds—the telepathic symbols used to communicate—have been scrambled by the last pole shift, the metaphoric collapse of the Tower of Babel or Pillar of God.

Thus we have to resort to reports from the mountain-top experiences of mystics, prophets, and shamans as our saviors: From Meru to Olympus to Sinai to Mount of Olives to the Oracles of Delphi.

Yet there is hope because not only are the pyramids and sacred site ruins still resonant with this truth but the crop circles seek to revitalize our "dead" memories as elegantly retold by graphic design artist Freddy Silva in *Secrets in the Fields: The Science and Mysticism of Crop Circles*.

More and more these cryptograms in cereal grains speak to our birthplace among the stars. Whether we examine Egyptian and Mayan hieroglyphs, the myths of Hopi Nation in the Southwestern United States, or crop circle images, we find a common theme in them all: the Hero Twins as binary star companions.

Indeed the idea that we are mirror-images of Christ is a major unifying theme of the *Gnostic Gospel of Thomas*. In that original text it is written that Jesus, a son of the Sun of God, had a twin brother named Judas Thomas Didymus, and even that is a play on words for twins. For both Thomas and Didymus mean twin, so Jesus supposedly had a twin brother named "twin-twin."

That is a dead giveaway from religion as to the fact that we are clones of Christ and come from the same star seed source in the Orion Nebula.

Robert Temple learned this truth from the Dogon tribe in Africa with respect to Nommo: "The parallels with Christ are extraordinary, even extending to Nommo being crucified on a tree, and forming a Eucharistic meal for humanity and then being resurrected." The genesis legends of creation are focused on salvation, thus begin and end with a divine pairing of Hero Twins: One saved and one sent to save the other's twin soul brother from a life of hell.

Indeed, the evidence is overwhelming for a Binary Soul Doctrine, or BSD.

Foremost authority on BSD, Peter Novak, documents in a trilogy of texts how he has rediscovered *The Lost Secret of Death, Our Divided Souls, and the Afterlife:* that if we live without "knowing" the reality of hells and heavens and how to navigate through these realms we get trapped in them once our soul—our conscious and unconscious mind—divides, separates, or splits from our physical body again at its time of death.

This is of course the focus of *The Tibetan Book of the Dead*. The chants, prayers are to awaken the soul to its situation post-mortem and send it to its eternal home in the sky, or heaven, or as I am suggesting back to the Orion Nebula: our original birthplace that we seek to mirror on earth with sacred site structures, myths, and rituals.

This truth then is what the Gospel of Thomas declared was the meaning to the admonition of Jesus "to make the two, one again." Our reward for doing so he said was clearly worth our best efforts for in the end "Whoever finds the interpretation of these sayings shall not taste death."

That is, upon death our soul's mind will not split itself in two again. Our intellect and affect, our thoughts and feelings, or memories, will not fragment and need to be retrieved from the "pit" we call hell. We can focus our whole integrated mind on returning to Twin Earth through the tunnel-of-light that will open to us as those near-death experiencers that I have interviewed have in fact shared with me is true.

The difference in life, and death, is all about Gnosis: Knowing the truth that will set us free!

In fact, the "pit" in the bottom of the Great Pyramid recreated the dark unknowing of Hades, the hell of unconsciousness; its aimless, mindless, soulless wanderings in the after-death realms, claimed author of the comprehensive text on this insight, *Decoding The Great Pyramid* by Peter Lemesurier.

So the rituals that took place in this specific pyramid complex with its pit, and the ascending Queen to King's Chamber were focused on resurrecting the "initiate" into remembrance. It was, in no uncertain terms, a shamanic soul retrieval or reincarnation technology that we also need to understand now.

Nor we do not want to lose our way in this earth's heavens that are floating freely within the magnetosphere, its fields of dreams, and forget to travel through the looking glass time-tunnel of light consciously that opens upon death into our mirror image earthlike twin world in the Orion Nebula.

Once more we see that our "failure to communicate" honestly with ourselves and each other as well as our binary twin star, soul double is the larger plan of salvation.

For we star children can use our lifeline to phone home telepathically!

Itzhak Bentov, a biomedical researcher, writes in *Stalking the Wild Pendulum: On the Mechanics of Consciousness*, "We may say now that in deep meditation the human being and the planet system start resonating at a very long wavelength of about 40,000 kilometers. It is the ideal medium for conveying a telepathic signal."

Our mind is the Mind of Mother Earth, but what happens to a planet and its people that do not linkup telepathically fast enough, achieve a unified field of mind, co-existence and harmony?

We suffer a severe electromagnetic pole shift due to the "unnatural disasters" we've created militarily that unbalanced the organic flow of light energy pulsating around and through the trunk of The World Tree. In the end, we find we have weakened the protective sheath of the magnetosphere that shielded our globe from the lethal doses of gamma-radiation mutations.

That is, we experience the purifying fire of the galactic and solar killing field. Indeed, we must restore environmental balance or we will be recycled in large numbers due to a nuclear catastrophe that triggers a war-ending pole shift is what the scriptures and shamans of every civilization tell us in one way or another.

This worst-case scenario has happened before according to the Sumerian scholar Zechariah Sitchin, declaring "The audacious idea of protecting a planet thermally by creating a shield of particles in its upper atmosphere is not as revolutionary as it seems. It was, I wrote in my 1976 book *The Twelfth Planet*, exactly the reason why the Anunnaki—'Those who from Heaven to Earth came'—had come here some 450,000 years ago from their planet Nibiru."

He adds: "On Nibiru -- 'Planet X' of our Solar System – the problem was the opposite one: Loss of internally generated heat due to a dwindling atmosphere, brought about by natural causes and nuclear wars. Nibiru's scientists, I wrote, concluded that the only way to save life on their planet was to create a shield of gold particles in their upper atmosphere. It was in search of the needed gold that the 'gods' of the ancient peoples had come to Earth."

For Earth, the showstopper is of course an all-out nuclear war, WWIII, known as the Battle of Armageddon, and that is why we focus on the City of Peace, Jerusalem, to see if the global scales of justice will be rebalanced by 2012—or we allow the wheels to fly off the axis of The World Tree.

Time will tell the tale once and for all very, very soon.

There are indeed many reliable sources not the least of which are the near-death experiences that dovetail with my research into Amerindian, Biblical, Egyptian and Mayan End-Time prophecies correlated with massive Earth Changes. One of the pioneers into NDE visions is Dr. Kenneth Ring, a social psychologist, who summarized the message of them to us as follows:

- "There is, first of all, a sense of having total knowledge, but specifically one is aware of seeing the entirety of the earth's evolution and history, from the beginning to the end of time."
- "The future scenario, however, is usually of short duration, seldom extending much beyond the beginning of the twenty-first century. The individual reports that … there will be an increasing incidence of earthquakes, volcanic activity and generally massive geophysical changes."
- "There will be resultant disturbances in weather patterns and food supplies. The world economic system will collapse, and the possibility of nuclear war of accident is very great but respondents are not agreed on whether a nuclear catastrophe will occur."
- "All of these events are transitional rather than ultimate, however, and they will be followed by a new era in human history, marked by human broth-

erhood, universal love and world peace. Though many will die, the earth will live."

In fact, according to some near-death experiencers that I have consulted such as Ned Dougherty, the cause of earth's catastrophes is consistent: "Every act of destruction of God's environment on Earth multiplied into destructive forces of nature—earthquakes, floods, pestilence." Equally, he was shown by a being of light in an Egyptian Temple while in what he saw was the Orion constellation that our planet's poles will shift or tilt. He reports, "A shifting of the Earth's axis will create dramatic climatic changes."

Dougherty says further, "During my 'death' experience, I had been told that humankind would evolve into a new and more spiritually transformed race of beings. Perhaps God would bestow upon mankind the ability to communicate telepathically, so that human beings could only then communicate honestly with each other."

In addition, we have the NDE testimony of Reverend Howard Storm who learned from beings of light hovering outside the center of a galaxy what our new heaven and new earth will be like for those alive then: "Everybody was a student of Nature, which they knew intimately and with which they could communicate, knowing the sensations and vibration of every part of creation. People explored outer space without moving an inch. People communicated telepathically with everyone on Earth and had relationships with intelligent beings on other worlds."

Yet Mayan scholar John Major Jenkins understands my immediate concerns clearly and forcefully, commenting in *Pyramid of Fire: The Lost Aztec Codex*: "The Greek writer Seneca … gives more details on the Babylonian World Age doctrine, saying that the world is alternately destroyed by flood or fire when the planets line up in Capricorn or Cancer. Such a statement implies that global destructions occur at the two extreme poles of the Great Year of precession."

Russian psychiatrist Immanuel Velikovsky, co-founder of the Hebrew University of Jerusalem, and author of *Worlds in Collision* declared destruction comes when "Two celestial bodies have been attracted one to each other. The inner masses of the Earth were pushed to the periphery. The Earth, with its rotational movement disturbed, started to warm."

Indeed, it is no coincidence that Mark Vidler in his book *The Star Mirror: The Extraordinary Discovery of The True Reflection Between Heaven and Earth* reports: "All the pyramids of the Old Kingdom have a shaft oriented to the polar region in the sky. This is one axis of the 'mill wheel' of the heavens and the arrival of a brilliant star at this point suggests that the heavenly axis is 'heating up.'"

Vidler adds: "In Hamlet's Mill, Giorgio de Santillana and Hertha von Deschend recover an abundance of evidence confirming the ancient preoccupation with this axis on the celestial sphere and its association with a predicted Earth Shift."

Specifically, Mark Vidler has performed years of careful research into the location of pyramids as gateways to stars. He correlates "stars to mountains," creating a crystal-clear sky-to-ground map that mirrors the geometry of the Great Pyramid. Interestingly, and prophetically, he reveals, "We are told that Polaris is an omen of global shift and have seen the ancient Egyptian murals depicting the sun taking a violent leap when it arrives on the raised limb of Orion."

That is to confirm, we will come under the cosmic ray gun of extremely intense Coronal Mass Ejections from our Sun. These galactic gamma-ray bursts are of concern to astrophysicist Paul LaViolette as he put forth in his book rightly titled *Earth Under Fire* because of interstellar dust clouds that are creating a thermal blanket around the Sun and cause it to overheat and explode violently in spasms of boiling plasma, CMEs, some of these aimed directly at Earth.

Adrian Gilbert understands as well, and reiterates, "As I have said, the southern star gate is of principle importance because it is also aligned with the center of our galaxy. What this means in practice is that on 21 December 2012, any person observing the Sun will also be looking directly toward the core of the Milky Way: the place where astronomers say there is a black hole with a mass some three hundred million times that of our Sun."

In summary, in the *Apocalypse of John*, also known as the *Book of Revelation*, we are warned that our world will be cast into a solar furnace, a "lake of fire" at the end-of-time. This scenario is in fact what Lou Famoso saw during his near-death, out-of-body experience to be true from the perspective of the Orion Nebula. He saw two balls of fire roar past him headed for our Sun. Then a HUGE CME erupted from it and headed straight for Earth. The result is an estimated 45 degree Pole Shift with simultaneous cataclysmic earthquakes, tsunamis, the sinking of old and rising of new continents, and the explosion of volcanoes on the Ring of Fire. So that we are not caught unawares, blind and dumb, an Angel he identified as Gabriel gave Mr. Famoso the following message to take back to us, and in closing I share that with you now:

"Look to Orion and you will know when the new world will come."

"The day will come when, after harnessing space, the winds, the tides, gravitation, we shall harness for God the energies of love. And, on that day, for the second time in the history of the world, humankind will have discovered fire."
—Pierre Teilhard de Chardin (1881-1955)

# # #

Dr. John Jay Harper is a clinical hypnotherapist and author of *Tranceformers: Shamans of the 21st Century*. He and his wife, Connie, live in Spokane, Washington. For more information, please refer to www.johnjayharper.com.

Ancient Code

By June-Elleni Lane

A book on ancient wisdom simply must include Art. Our use of artwork is in the human psyche and has been active since our ancestors did cave paintings at least 40,000 years ago. It is a way to manifest our future plans by creating an image of our intention. With focused intention the image we produce consistently broadcasts the intent to all who see it; consciously, subconsciously and even unconsciously. This is, therefore a very subtle and powerful way to create and manifest anything we can imagine. Remember nothing is built today without drawing out the plans first. So it makes perfect sense to draw out a plan for manifesting your life goals.

Because artwork has been around for so long, we seem to have forgotten its power, purpose and its real value. Real value that is, not in terms of £ and $ for example to purchase an original Picasso, but real value in terms of broadcasting energy.

I personally would not wish to have the energy of a Picasso painting from his blue period in my home, whatever its perceived cash value. These paintings really broadcast a sad and depressive energy, due to this period in his life.

This idea of art broadcasting energy is central to my work with Mandalas. My book *Mandala The Art Of Creating Future* is a simple "how to" book, for guiding beginners and non-artistic people as well as artists to draw out their intentions and use the pictures they make to manifest their intent. This very simple process can be leaned fairly quickly and used easily once you know how.

I use art in other forms in my work to help people to connect to source energy. I am certain the saying "a picture paints a thousand words" is the best eulogy I can give.

I started using art in this way because I concluded that art is a helpful way to trigger and develop the right brain hemisphere. When I discovered Roger Sperry split brain research that won him the Nobel prize 1981, something lit up in my mind, I was convinced this was an important and helpful way to look at ourselves and the way we function, or sometimes don't function as well as we could. He suggests the following brain lateralization is true in most cases…

Linear reasoning and language such as grammar and vocabulary are often lateralized to the left hemisphere of the brain. Whereas, additional language functions, such as intonation and accentuation, are often lateralized to the right hemisphere. Functions such as the processing of vision and sound, spatial manipulation, facial perception, and artistic ability seem to be functions of the right hemisphere also.

Other integrative functions, including arithmetic, binaural sound localization, instinct and emotions, seem more bilaterally controlled.

Generally however this seems to be the overall conclusion –

Left hemisphere functions	Right hemisphere functions
analytical	holistic
language	sound
logical	intuitive
calculative math	estimative math
exact	context
knowledge	wisdom

Understanding these functions as two distinct and separated areas, helped me to learn how to trigger right-brain participation deliberately, it helped me use right-brain functions when I wanted to connect with my psychic ability or intuition and also when I wanted to control any fears or phobias.

It has been a life-changing realization for me and very helpful in teaching others to change their lives for the better. You can read more about the work I do connecting through art in my books or on my website www.psychicartwork.com.

Finally if you wish to experience a different way of looking at art, using the right-brain hemisphere, try this experiment for yourself. Log onto www.psychicartworks.com/joy.html to find my Mandala depicting "JOY."

Now stare at the image ... your first experience will be left-brain thinking. What does this image look like, what does it remind me of, what color is it and why. What's this all about? Then I ask you to change your thoughts, to the following:-

Instead of sending out your consciousness to explore the image, draw the image into you through your eyes; asking how does it make me feel? Connect with your body and explore how it makes you feel. Connect with what's happening within.

Then just to become even more aware, change the way you're thinking back and forwards from what does it look like, to how do I feel about it and enjoy ... Pure Alchemy!

# # #

June-Elleni Laine was a fashion designer and business-woman for 20 years. For the past 18 years she has been a shamanic/psychic artist and clairvoyant. She is a qualified Ayurvedic health educator and massage therapist. She has been a tutor at London's College of Psychic Studies for 8 years and leads courses, workshops and retreats in UK, Europe and Turkey, she hosts a radio chat show on myspiritradio.com. She is often seen in the media in various magazines and on news and documentaries on National TV and also at MBS festivals. She has a mission to move beyond the limited perspective of the five senses and the ego, helping people to reconnect through art! She is the author of *The Art of Being ... Psychic* and *Mandala The Art Of Creating*.

If Christianity Becomes Irrelevant in 2012, Will Jesus as Well?

By Janice Manning, Editor, *The Kolbrin Bible*

Many of late believe that 2012 represents a peaceful transition from a violent period in modern history to a more gentle, evolved and compassionate future. That would be nice, but if the transition is not so peaceful, will the religions of the world, which we have come to trust to give us peace in times of turmoil, survive the transition?

What do the ancients tell us about 2012 and this transition? By all accounts, they say it will be painful, so much so that it will test us as a species. Likewise, our institutions and beliefs will undergo a similar trial by fire. Like us, it will be their first, and for many, their last.

Christianity will certainly be tried, as it is the dominant belief system of the Western, capitalized world. If Christianity as a faith fails this coming test, where does that leave Christians, as well as non-Christians, who likewise admire the teachings of Jesus Christ?

Rather than looking to the present or the future for an answer, a more reliable measure is human history, or more specially, what the ancients foresaw for what will become our own history.

This is not a radical concept, as we do it ourselves. For example, we openly speculate about what life will be like at the end of this century, given changing weather patterns, rising sea levels, overpopulation and so on. In doing so, we're creating messages in bottles and throwing them into the sea of time.

Eventually, they'll wash up on the beaches frequented by our decedents, and they'll offer such pithy observations as "good luck with cleaning up the massive debts and the debilitated biosphere we created for you, but please try to like us anyway."

Fortunately for us, our ancients did not send us hydrocarbon waste. Just knowledge, and it comes to us mainly in the forms of folklore and prophecy.

Like messages in bottles set adrift in the sea of time millennia ago, a few have managed to wash upon the shores of our time, and we have used these prophetic messages from the ancients to gain awareness of the natural tribulations we'll soon face.

In this manner, we can likewise learn from the ancients how they overcame similar tribulations, and one that drives to the heart of this discussion is: if Christianity becomes irrelevant in 2012, will Jesus as well?

While there are many ancient cultures and wisdom texts that could address this discussion in general terms, only one of these ancient cultures offers the specificity through its ancient wisdom texts. That culture is the ancient Celts - Pagans who embraced harmony with the Earth and the teachings of Jesus with an equal passion for understanding.

Perhaps the ancient Celts viewed the teachings of Jesus with a more practical view, one beyond the simple message of compassion for the weak and infirm. Like other early Christians, they rejecting him as a god, and for this, as well their close ties to nature, they suffered terribly in the burning, political winds of the emerging paternal trinity belief system.

Did the ancient Celts veer away from the truth as promulgated by power elites, or did they remain steadfast in a simpler vision of what Jesus had taught them? One that calls us to the noblest goal of human spiritual evolution and could be defined in a modern sense by Marshall Masters, author of *Godschild Covenant and 2012 Wisdom of The Elohim*.

"What Judaism, Christianity and Islam consistently fail to understand about Rabbi Yeshua Ben Yosef (Jesus the Christ) is the essence of the man and his message. One that can be easily stated in four simple words – stop thinking like slaves." – Marshall Masters

With this assumption, the relevant question becomes patently obvious. Does this modern view of the "essence" of Jesus expressed by Marshall Masters, somehow fit with what the ancient Celts believed? Yes it does, and proof of this connection is found in *The Kolbrin Bible* - a newly-revealed, 2-part wisdom text that dates back to the turbulent years following the Hebrew Exodus from Egypt.

The first part of this secular wisdom text was written by Egyptian Scholars, and the second part was penned by Celtic Priests in the early years following the death of Jesus. What is stunning is that there are lengthy accounts by a Celtic biographer in *The Kolbrin Bible*. They are found in the *The Britain Book*, and they clearly demonstrate a familiarity between the biographer, Jesus and many of his inner circle.

BRT:2:1 This is the true record of events concerning Jesus, son of Joseph and Mary, which we have received by the hands of several who have lived within the circle of His Light, and more especially from one who is our earthly father in the faith. He being not the least among the articulate ones who knew Jesus, and a person of no mean estate, both in the distant land from whence he came and in this more virile land.

The Celts' "earthly father in the faith" spoken of here was Joseph of Arimethea, uncle to Yeshua ben Yosef on his mother's side. Joseph came to the British Isles approximately three years after the death of Yeshua and brought his sacred writings with him, sacred writings that would upset Christians and atheists alike.

The very existence of *The Kolbrin Bible* cuts the wrong way with secular atheists because it provides evidence that Jesus was in fact a real person and not a figment of folklore, as many maintain.

Conversely, *The Kolbrin Bible* cuts in the opposite direction, and with equal annoyance, for many Christians. This is because it documents how early pagans and converts clearly rejected the notion that Jesus was a god. Nonetheless, they deeply loved him and were inspired by him as a teacher and prophet.

BRT:2:3 In the *Sacred Books of the Idewin* it is written: "The Son of Man is the shepherd of men and we know how diligently a shepherd tends his flocks."

Jesus came not as a shepherd to drive, but as one bearing a guiding lantern to show the way. It is also written: "The Son of Man is the deliverer of men," and while we know from what we have to be delivered, those who lived in His land misunderstood the meaning.

BRT:3:49 It came to pass, at this time, that many said that Jesus was the Messiah, but this was a manifest falsehood. Jesus, the son of Joseph and Mary, was an inspired prophet, a teacher who held the hand of God and there had been others before Him. His mother was a decent woman; both ate food as humans do. Mary did not set herself up as a goddess, neither did she preach.

BRT:3:50 It is of no moment to those who are not Jews whether Jesus was the heralded Messiah or not, so believe as you will, but were He born of a Holy Ghost and not of Joseph, then He did not fulfill the prophesy. Men step outside the bounds of truth in their beliefs, but this, too, is of little moment unless they impose their beliefs on others.

The death and destruction brought up the ancient Celts for these beliefs was horrendous and the Glastonbury Abbey where the texts of the original Great Book, from which *The Kolbrin Bible* was compiled, were nearly all destroyed, along with the Abbey by command of a British King, acting at the behest of the Church.

Yet, the surviving Celtic priests managed to save enough of the texts, and they tell us how the teachings of Jesus could once again flourish in a post-2012 existence, well after the end of Christianity as we know it today. These specific writings are contained in Celtic Texts of the *Coelbook*, the second part of *The Kolbrin Bible*.

The first thought we must keep in mind as we examine these ancient writings is that 2012 and the years beyond will be like a spiritual and technological tsunami.

In a sense, it will strip away the false structures and roadways of commerce created by conventional theology, so the business of religion will cease. As with the Black Plague in Europe which spawned the Renaissance, people will be searching elsewhere and within, for the hope of a brighter future. One filled with truth and enlightenment.

Given that 2012 will strip away millennia of theological asphalt, it will expose fertile soil that has lain dormant for far too long. Buried deep in this ancient soil are the seeds of the teachings of Jesus.

Free to bask in the sunlight of a new future, these will poke through the shattered debris of theological asphalt as the sprouts reach towards the sun. Free at last, they shall grow mightily. Not because of the fear of a God, but the love of a concept. That we stop thinking like slaves, as Marshall Masters interprets the essence of Jesus. Consider this; one who thinks like a slave has only two futures – that of a downtrodden field slave or that of a pampered house slave.

Obviously, either fate negates our most precious gift. The God-given freedom of free will —the right to choose.

The Celts treasured this gift, and they loved Jesus because they saw in him a wise, kindred teacher in spirit with themselves. However, it was not love at first sight.

When Joseph of Arimethea first brought the teachings to Britain, the Celts and their Druid priests, who were lovers of the land and nature, were skeptical of the newcomers, even though the king had granted them a stretch of land, on which to live.

Joseph's solution was to let the land speak for itself.

BRT:1:15 Now, when the strangers were granted the land, the Druthin disputed this with the king and said that they wanted a divine sign that their gods approved. Ilyid said, "Give me but half a year." At the witnessing of this, the Druthin set up a holistone, and Ilyid struck his staff into the soil to mark the covenant.

BRT:1:16 The following Eve of Summer there was a gathering and it was found that a small green shoot was coming up from the ground beside the staff, which was an offshoot of the staff. The king decreed that this was a sign that the land accepted the strangers, but these took it as a sign that what they taught fell on fertile ground and would take root.

Indeed, both interpretations did come to pass. After some time, both the land and the people welcomed the strangers and their teachings, although the latter came with some compromises that made the teachings acceptable to both sides.

BRT:4:12 Joseph, our father, said, "I have not come to batter down your house of hope, for it has many pleasing features, even as ours. So let us not disagree, but take the best from both and, discarding what is less good, fashion something of value to all. Let us weigh one thing against the other, rejecting that, which less clearly shows the way."

BRT:4:16 The Chief of All Druthin said, "Often have I thought on this. All men are alike in nature and all aspire to the same goal. All seek to make the same journey's end; only the route differs. Therefore, let us not argue whether men should follow your road or mine, but find between us a path better than either."

A path that was "better than either" was found, and upon it, the ancient Celts studied and adopted the teachings of Jesus, which Joseph of Arimethea had brought to them.

What they learned and admired about Jesus was that he was a man of honor, strength, determination and courage, who was full of love and compassion.

They saw him as one who hallowed all of God's creation, just as they did, yet at the same time did not tolerate hypocrisy and intolerance.

BRT:3:12 A teacher of the Jewish way said to Jesus, "If God is so great and all knowing, why does He not strike down the wrongdoer? Why does He withhold His justifiable wrath when the wicked man swallows up the man who follows the path of goodness? Is he not the God of justice?" Jesus replied, "Justice is not a thing of the time. Though the mills of God grind slowly, they grind to perfection. Life itself metes out justice. The justice of God adjusts the injustice of men. Were this not so, I would not have come."

BRT:3:24 A man asked, "Where is God?" Jesus took a piece of bread and gave it to the man, saying, "Take this and hold it." Then He said, "Put out the other hand." He poured a little water on the upturned palm and said, "Now you have felt the power of God, for without His spirit in the bread and in the water, these would not exist for you. Split a billet of wood, and God will be there. Lift up a stone, and you will find Him."

To the nature-loving Celts, who could access the spiritual world without the fetters of dogma and see the Creator's spirit in all of nature, Britain 3:24 fell in nicely with their beliefs.

The Celts had their own gods, so they did not see Jesus as a god. Instead, they saw him as a wise, but humble, loving teacher and prophet. Therefore, they were pleased to learn that Jesus did not consider himself a god. In fact, his own people had asked him often if he was God or one with God. Here is his answer on one occasion.

BRT:3:13 Jesus was then asked if He was one with God, and He answered, "It is not in Me to state that, which I know to be untrue, and truly there can be but one God alone. Because I have been granted visions and insight into things unseen and unknown to other men, what manner of man would I be did I claim equality with God? I have spoken only that which I am bidden. I have said, 'Worship God who is My Father and your Father.' Does this then raise Me above other men? I have proclaimed all men My brothers, and if I have said I am even as God, then truly I have raised them up also. Yet, this they cannot see, or is it that they fear the burden of their own godhood?"

BRT:3:29 Jesus taught that there are things, which should be approached with humility of spirit, they are: holiness, wisdom and nobility. Humility bestows upon the soul the benefit of harmony and attunement ...

Going hand in hand with humility is an unshakable love for all things. Therefore finally, the teachings that resonated the best with the Celts and will serve us best in the coming transition of 2012 were about Jesus' love and respect for nature and humanity. These will surely be the first fruits of a New Earth to break through the shattered asphalt of the old in shining beauty, like the first flowers of spring. Here are a few of them.

BRT:3:21 Who is most praiseworthy for his goodness, the son of a rich man or the son of a poor man? The rich son gives only what he himself has been given, so surely it is the son of the poor man, for he has overcome the temptations of poverty and satisfied the cry of hungry mouths with the earnings of his own labor. It is the poor who help the poor, for the rich help themselves.

BRT:3:22 There are those who fast for the sake of Heaven, but Jesus said it were better did they devote themselves to learning the scriptures and to good works for the sake of Heaven. Yet, it is useless to merely read the scriptures, for unless they be taken into the heart and lived by, then they are things of little value and use. The value of all sacred writings lies in what people do with them. More important still is what the scriptures do to the people.

BRT:3:27 One day, Jesus and those with Him came upon an old man playing with childish things. A bow and arrow-bearing huntsman passing by mocked him, saying, "Behold the old man playing as a child." Jesus called him over and said, "Do you always keep your bow bent, the string under stress?" "Of course not" replied the huntsman. "To do so would be foolish, for the bow would become useless were it not unbent from time to time." Jesus said, "Just so is it with the old man, and you should know better."

BRT:3:57 Jesus saw a man ill-treating a horse, and He rebuked him for his cruelty to a dumb animal. The man became angry and said, "This is my beast." Jesus said, "You are wrong, it is God's creature, and I, as His servant, am here to protect it. For no man can wholly own any living creature except it be in the name of The Great God of Life."

These are just some of the teachings of Jesus found in *The Kolbrin Bible*. Those who revere them as the ancient Celts did, without dogma or conditions, will see them flourish into a bright, new Earth full of life, love and promise. In essence, their message in a bottle sent to us across the stormy seas of time is simple to grasp in the modern sense.

If Christianity becomes irrelevant in 2012, the teachings of Jesus will become more relevant than ever before.

# # #

Janice Manning co-authored *Planet X Forecast* and *2012 Survival Guide* and is the editor of *The Kolbrin Bible,* a wisdom text dating back some 3600 years. Her analyses of the historical accounts regarding previous Planet X flybys in this ancient secular text were instrumental in correlating those accounts to similar accounts in the *Torah* (Old Testament).

Considered a leading authority on *The Kolbrin Bible*, she is recognized in the 2007 edition of *Who's Who of American Women* for her work. She is also a yowusa.com web site co-founder.

2012 Is About Dark Workers Too

By Marshall Masters, ©2009

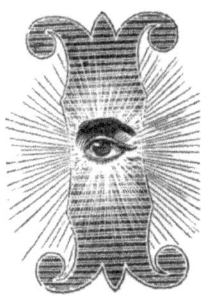

Throughout the history of humankind, there have always been the friends of the species and those who simply view it as a resource. One they are free to exploit at will and in as disruptive a manner as they see fit to serve their own needs.

These foes of humanity do not view humankind as a sentient species, but merely as a resource: whereas they see themselves as the true sentient, if not godlike species. Consequently, they can only be seen as all knowing, all rightful and all wise by their obedient vassals.

Vassals so weak in their own connection with the creator that they choose to bond with a force their fearful minds can more easily understand. They in turn, serve to act out the wishes of those who would exploit humanity for intentions, which run counter to the right of every species. To progress along a more enlightened path towards the creator.

Does it matter that these foes are of this world or another? Certainly not, for their agendas all produce the same outcome. The enslavement of a noble species destined to seek a higher purpose in the mind of the creator thereby making them the convenient chattels of a self-omnipotent force of beings, possessing a marginally greater technology.

It is with great concern that all humans should seek to protect their species from these usurpers of evolution, regardless of whether they emanate — from within or without.

These usurpers are the final test humanity must overcome, and such a victory, though costly, is well worth the price. Paid with the blood of loved ones and the treasure of fruitful labors, the need is universal for humankind: to join together as brothers and sisters, as one species united. In this, comes a singular freedom from tyranny that ensures evolution. It is a small price and one that all must forever be mindful of.

Pay it honestly, and the species will evolve. Shirk the payment, and it will not. This is the simple duality of the sentient evolution of humanity. Such has always been the same for every sentient life form imaginable, scattered throughout the heavens on worlds so distant, they are far flung to the outer edges of human imagination.

In this knowing, humanity is not alone as it shares a greater hope of evolved life throughout the cosmos. To come together as one, so the one may join with the enlightened many.

Opposed to this plan, reviling it, and what it portends, are the dark workers, and their numbers are many. Yet, they are not the whole, nor even a fair portion of it. They are the few, but their bitter poison is perverse and can easily spread throughout the body of a species, just as microbial entities can extinguish the life of a gleeful newborn, seeking the full growth of its age.

To ignore the signs of these dark workers is to invite their poison into the body of the species whole: to allow them to corrupt and thereby cannibalize that which is not theirs to own.

To celebrate awareness is the sweet fruit of participation. The act of becoming brothers and sisters in the one, for the noble goal of sparking the evolved steps of an enlightened species, closer to the mind of the creator.

However, do not celebrate your ambitions so loudly and with such great fervor, that your jubilees drown out the footsteps of those who lurk amongst and about you, intent on holding you down. Down to where they may profit from your misery as they methodically extract the essence of your life and your freedom from you.

Yes, there are dark workers too, so one must always be mindful, yet not unbalanced.

To step closer to the mind of the creator requires the songs of love that spin the visions, which draw us onward. Conversely, the siren call of those envious of that vision must be heard with equal clarity for theirs is the complement of the universal duality of evolution. One drawing us high, as the other pulls us low.

Be wise in your observations and sparing in your judgment so that you may better distinguish the differences between true light workers and those proclaiming a false purpose for the benefit of a hidden few.

Be discerning in the messages you allow yourself to receive, and trust your own inner guides. In this, you shall find the true path of the light worker, as one seeking to commune with others in the mind of God, knowing this to be the only truth path.

Those bent in the dark worker ways, will utter right-sounding words and with great eloquence, but their messages will always be the same in the end — to trust elsewhere but yourself. Do this, and your misplaced trust shall become a silent thread to their dark masters and they will use it to bond you to their aims and intentions.

Listen to everything, but only hear yourself. This is the path of the light worker and all those who seek to follow the path of the light worker. A path, the dark workers can only see from a far distance and with a vision clouded by their own envious hates and mistrusts.

Be not like them for they draw power not by their acts, but by robbing you of your own connection to the creator. They are the parasites of the human soul, and they know their trade all too well, so do not think you can toy with them successfully. Such naïve expressions of ego inevitably become the foolish grist of their grinding mills.

Walk the pure path and seek your own council in all things before drawing near to anyone or anything, no matter what is professed. Within you is the Creator, and the connection is your guide. It is your shield. It is your destiny.

#

Marshall Masters is an author, publisher, media guest, internet radio host and founder of Your Own World Books. A former CNN science features news producer and U.S. Army public information officer; he specializes in Planet X and 2012 research and founded the yowusa.com web site in 1999.

He is a former CNN Science Features field producer and produces the informational and self-help videos featured on this site, and through the Youtube.com/Yowbooks channel.

His published works include *Planet X Forecast* and *2012 Survival Guide, 2012 Wisdom of The Elohim, Godschild Covenant: Return of Nibiru* and *The Kolbrin Bible*.

The Key to the Code

By Brian Mayne

The Ancient Code, and key to life, has always been known to an enlightened few throughout history. And although the Code is not a secret, and is in fact woven into the great truths of all ancient wisdoms, it is still a mystery to most and must be discovered by each person for their self through their own individual quest for truth. The key to the code is balance.

Balance is the prime natural-law that not only governs the infinite diversity of life, but also helps to produce it in the first place. The whole of creation is a dynamic balance of opposites, an interactive dance of polarities; of spirit and mater, male and female, negative and positive.

Being truly universal, the principle of balance goes to the heart of nature and applies equally to a single atom or entire solar system, an individual person or whole civilization. The same fundamental principle of balance that keeps particles whizzing within atoms and planets spinning around stars, also propels us through our life. When we are balanced our life works well. When we are unbalanced worlds collide and we fall apart.

Ancient people knew this intuitively and lived to a natural rhythm in harmony and balance with the Code. However mankind has grown increasingly unbalanced in the way that we live. Controlled by the clock and out of step with the seasons, our civilization is driving people apart from Nature and resulting in the destruction of our world around us.

People everywhere are now realizing with growing concern that the extreme changes in our climate are the result of humanity affecting the natural balance of our planet. Likewise, the wildly fluctuating economic climate is the result of our lopsided ways of living. The rise of consumerism, culture of waste and unbalanced business practices where profit is put before people has created a false sense of worth in the world with the latest financial storm or political crises being just another symptom of a sick system.

It cannot be ignored. The signs of our unbalanced living patterns are all around us; in our weather, our economy, our diet and health, the way we treat each other, the value we place on things and our worship of celebrity.

History teaches by example that civilizations rise to greatness by being balanced, and fall to their destruction when they become overly unbalanced.

Let us not wait for our civilisation to completely fall, crash and burn before we remember the lessons of balance. Let us not wait for politicians to pass a policy or business to create the profit-plan.

In earnest, let each of us live the Ancient Code now for ourselves and regain the balance in our life. By each of us seeking to be our best and have balance in ourselves, so we live a balanced life, and add to the collective balance in our family, community and society. In this way we can each help to heal our world.

Be the Code

To have balance you must first have opposites. Every yin must have a yang, a positive for the negative, male and female. Life is truly a mirror. The inner drives the outer. The measure of balance in your life will be a reflection of the balance in yourself. And while life is complex, with countless different balancing points, the essence of achieving life-balance will always fundamentally begin by finding balance between your self and Self.

In the 11th century the Sufi mystic Jelaluddin Rumi observed;

> Awhile, as wont may be, self I did claim;
> True Self I did not see, but heard its name.

> I, being self confined, Self did not merit,
> till leaving self behind did Self inherit.

We each have two selves: a high Self, as written above with a capital S, and a low self, indicated with a lower case s.

Our high Self descends from spirit to guide us by way of inspiration and empathy. It is infinite; the seat of our soul and source of our divinity. Representing all of our finest Humanitarian qualities our high Self is our connection to the All. It is the essence of who we truly are; our well-spring of unconditional love.

In balance, our low self ascends from our animal ancestry and encapsulates all of our evolutionary and genetic traits. It is finite; programmed for survival; moves away from pain; coordinates our automatic body systems; operates through instinct, fear and primal emotions; and is the home of our ego.

Get the Balance Right

From the moment we are born both our high Self and low self are present within us to varying degrees, and like the yin and yang, and are intended to work together in a balanced partnership of interactive harmony.

Our high Self is created to lead. It is associated with our right-brain and processes the qualities of imagination and inspiration. It shines with a brilliance that illuminates a path for our low self to follow. Our low self is an effective "doer," it is associated with our left-brain and is best suited to managing and organizing repetitive tasks and actions.

When our two selves are united in balanced harmony we become our integrated "True Self" and thereby live our best life. From our high Self right-brain we lead with a sense of awareness, vision and purpose, while in balance with our low self left-brain we effectively plan and manage our journey.

However, when we become unbalanced and our low self seizes control, lacking the qualities of vision and heart, it becomes lost, uncaring and selfish. When we live from our low self we become excessive, reactive, and driven by fear to grasp at food, shelter and clothing. But because the ego or low self always hungers for more, no amount is ever enough, we violate the Ancient Code, and destroy our world.

Know your Self – Live the Code

Our high Self and low self are like flip sides of a coin - you can't have one without the other. While the low self doubts, our high Self believes. The low self looks backwards through past experience, while the high Self looks forwards through the gift of imagination. The high Self moves towards comfort, the low self is driven by fear to move away from pain.

Both sets of qualities are essential for our wellbeing. No aspect of the low self is truly negative when in natural balance with the high Self, life and circumstance. Fear protects us; past experience informs us; and doubt enables us to be discerning.

Only when unbalanced and excessive does our low self cause damage as self-doubt spirals down into a crises of confidence and on to some form of self-sabotage.

While our high Self is fluid and exists in the moment, our low self is grounded and becomes rooted in established beliefs, fixed attitudes and repeated behavior, all of which contribute to form our sense of personality or self. The more fixed in beliefs and hardened in attitudes our low self becomes, the more it overshadows or blocks the light from our high Self. Our ego or false-self becomes dominant, clouds the window on our soul, and we become blind to the best part of us.

There is an ancient Indian tale about 3 blind men who encounter an elephant for the first time. One inspects the trunk and concludes the beast is like a big snake. The next finds a leg and decides he is sensing some kind of tree. The third grabs the tail and thinks he is holding a rope.

What's the moral of the story? We all see life from a different perspective depending on our past experience and beliefs, and are all blind in some way, especially about the ultimate Truth of our Self.

Evolving from self to Self

In ancient times it was believed that Gnosis - knowledge of the self - was the highest of all wisdoms. Knowing your self - your own beliefs, attitudes and behaviors, helps you live in balance, in all that you do, and thereby create your best results.

However, if we are blind to our self, unconscious of our own low self habits and attitudes, if we violate the Ancient Code and become unbalanced then we repeatedly stumble into the same old pitfalls and mistakes. While there are many paths in life that can be taken, some less challenging than others, and many that are well meant and spiritually intended, the qualities of the low self and ego are fundamentally the same. The low self is constantly moving away from some form of pain or other, whether real or just imagined, in both situations and relationships, and therefore never truly finds lasting happiness.

For the person who is driven by their low self ego there is no true rest, they are always on edge in some way, wanting, worrying or warring. There may be great achievements, rewards and accolades, but the real goal of life is not accumulation, conquest or even accomplishment, but rather peace and happiness - to live in harmony and balance with our self, humanity, and nature.

The Journey Home

The prime purpose of our life, the "big goal" that we are each born with, is to re-unite our self with our Self, low with high, like two partners reuniting that had grown apart.

When we marry our low self with our high Self, we merge our qualities and, through the complementary difference, create "synergy of self." We become our True Self.

Courage balanced with consideration. Ego balanced by spirit and love balanced by natural fear, allow us to be fluid, spontaneous in the moment and flow in harmony with the current of creation to live in balance with peace and abundance.

By making the two One, bringing our high Self and low self together into

One integrated True Self, we are able to live our life with spirit and create our chosen desires while still maintaining our balance in life.

Conscious Self-Integration, the True Path

Only in this way, by bringing our high Self and low self together, to become our True Self do we truly live by the Ancient Code and are we fully empowered for life's journey - able to find meaning in the good as well as the so called bad; the desired as well as the un-intentioned.

Making the two One, is the journey that all humanity has been traveling since the birth of consciousness. Gradually moving from; the true nature of humanity which is largely fear-driven, ego based and self-centered, to; the nature of True Humanity – leading from our True Self by being purpose led, heart-centered, and selfless.

If life is a journey, then surly the true goal of life is not to reach the journey's end as quickly as possible, nor collect the most souvenirs. The true goal is to make the most of the trip, having the most fun and create the most happiness along the way.

This is not the type of fun and happiness that come just from experiencing happy events, for we will all meet rocks of disappointment, chasms of despair and pools of sorrow along our path.

The happiness that springs from your True Self is totally free and abundant. It is the happiness that is independent of happy events. It is the happiness and peace-of-mind that come from learning to evolve your small self, find your great Self, and integrate the two to become your True Self.

Living the Code

Achieving "life-balance" is not a static point in time or space - such as the balance on a set of scales. "Life-balance," whether in a particle or a person, is active and dynamic. In life the natural point of focus is always shifting, like the rotation of seasons or swing of a pendulum shifting between poles, from the yin to the yang, creation and destruction, negative to positive. The measure of swing to the right is the measure of swing to the left.

What you may need to do today to achieve balance may be completely different from what you may need to do tomorrow. Nothing really remains the same. There is no finite balance point. All of life is either green and growing or ripe and rotten. This is true for plants, particles or people; without change we would each sink into a shrinking comfort-zone of sameness and the Universe would freeze in time.

The principle of "interactive-balance" sits at the very essence of creation. It is the balanced interaction of energies that forms particles. Particles whiz around each other in balanced orbits of attraction and repulsion to create atoms. Atoms in turn create molecules, worlds and everything in them, including us.

Modern scientific breakthroughs now prove what ancient universal wisdom has always maintained; that Reality is a symphony of interacting vibrations all harmoniously creating life.

Balance is the song that Nature instinctively sings. Each aspect of life joins in the tune and adds to the rhythm – a free-flowing melody of evolution. And while mankind is a life-member of the band, he has increasingly gone solo to sing his own tune, drowning out everyone else in the process.

Blessed with the divine ability of freewill and imagination, Humankind has been able to consciously create His chosen reality. Our evolving consciousness has enabled us to make nature serve our every need; as we learnt to fashion sticks into tools, forests into fields, piles of rocks into houses, and propel rockets to the moon.

The inner drives the outer. You are part of reality. You give off vibrations, creating attractions, and are playing your part in the orchestra. Each thought you think produces an energy that creates a vibration, like plucking a string. A repeated thought becomes a belief and is like a constant strumming. Through our thoughts, words and deeds we not only add music to the great song of life, we can also ride the rhythm to create our own tune.

Live by the Ancient Code and be your True Self and the song of your life will flow with the spontaneous harmony of natures rhythms?

# # #

An inspirational speaker, author and teacher, Brian Mayne, creator of the world-leading achievement system Goal Mapping, shares eternal truths on success in simple language and his own powerful life experience.

Born into a traveling fun-fair family with a nomadic childhood Brian left school early with no qualifications and a poor education. When the family business failed in the UK recession of the late 1980s he lost what seemed like everything; his income, his home and his marriage. He was 29 years old, a million pounds in debt, and still relatively unable to read or write.

It was at this seemingly low point that Brian discovered the keys to success: that you can change your life by changing your thoughts and feelings about it. Using simple but powerful techniques Brian learned to hold positive thoughts by setting goals and through them gradually transformed himself and his life.

Now an international speaker on success, Brian empowers hundreds of thousands of people around the world with his unique systems for success. "Goal Mapping" in particular has helped people from all walks of life to turn their dreams into realities.

Brian's acclaimed books, audios, videos and live presentations have won universal praise for their clarity and effectiveness, helping not only individuals to achieve their aims and goals, but also leading organizations such as Siemens, Microsoft, and British Telecom.

A UK National Training Award recipient, author of four books in eight languages, and creator of the Seven Magic Keys children's development programme, Brian is closer than ever to achieving his core goal of helping to lift seven million lives with his success systems.

To discuss how Brian can enliven your event, team or entire organization, call 01983 852 815, email enquiries@liftinternational.com or visit our website www.liftinternational.com.

Leonardo da Vinci and The Mayan Code

By Steve Mitchell

There are so many places that I could choose to begin this article from, that even finding a suitable title has proved to be a bit of a bugbear. For example, are the King and the land one? What is the message of the Grail? Will the world end in 2012?

The long and the short of it is that, whichever way you look at it, there is an amazing code, a pattern or blueprint if you like, that is not only programmed into the structure and functioning of every living thing but results in the same mathematics and science that governs the movements of the planets and galaxies in the universe itself. It is the same code whose product was the precise placement of this planet on which we live in relation to its sun in such a way that life itself was possible in the first place.

Much has been written in recent years about Leonardo da Vinci, initially propagated in 1982 by the publication of *The Holy Blood and The Holy Grail* by Michael Baigent, Richard Leigh, and Henry Lincoln and more recently accelerated by Dan Brown's novel *The Da Vinci Code*. They all focus on a number of paintings which allegedly show certain graphical references to a cup or grail, the relationship between Jesus and Mary Magdalene and the identity and gender of one of the disciples, prompting thoughts about a sacred bloodline and the hidden secret behind religious doctrines.

Drawn towards the end of the 15th century by the artist da Vinci, his study, Vitruvian Man holds much more esoteric wisdom than this that is as yet still untapped.

It is a study of form and proportion based on an illustration of the perfect man that first appeared in the treatise *De Architectura* by the Roman architect Vitruvius. That it is a "perfect" man is really important here, for, as the field of anthropometry notes, none of us are perfectly proportioned and all display individual variations on this theme. However, at this point, one thing is perfectly true. That is, were any of us to lie on the ground and spin our body around our center, the extremities of our fingers and toes would describe a perfect circle. If we were to do the same thing standing up but spin ourselves horizontally, that is around the axis that runs from the top of our head to the bottom of our feet, then again the tips of our fingers would describe a perfect circle. If we were to be able to spin ourselves vertically like doing a handstand with our hands held high, over a bar set at approximately our navel region, again our finger tips and toes would describe another perfect circle. Combining these three circles in all three dimensions, as if in a centrifugal machine, spinning about the exact center of our body, all of us would describe with our extremities a perfect sphere.

This then is the primary geometric structure that our body conforms to, a perfect sphere, and leads me to note that in our lifetime we live within that sphere and if you were to take a series of snapshots thoughout our lives, with the centre of the snapshot always being on the centre of our body, and combine those snapshots in three dimensions it would again result in the very same perfect sphere.

Truly then, we live our entire lives confined physically within this perfect circle and by extension so does everything, every plant, every animal in the universe, and that circle is defined by the proportional parts of each element of the being. If we were to take the orbits of each planet and spin those around their central axis of rotation again the result would be a perfect sphere. The same goes for the galaxy and so forth.

This leads me to observe that, as da Vinci believed, the workings of the human body are essentially analogous to the workings of the universe itself and that spiritual existence is not only symbolized by the circle but in every way is circular and, in the three dimensional sense, spherical. In reality we can note more than this at this point, as, to be able to describe a sphere, a body has to move through time and space, thus spiritually and physically incorporating at least the next dimension of time. In a sense, this sphere also represents the coincidental potential for that body to be in any part of that space, which collapses into the actual when it is observed at, or from a specific point in time and space.

This may seem like just some half baked, modern day "quantum theory" but evidence of the observation and belief in a circular universe can be found in the archeological debris from the dawn of civilization, and beyond.

It is thought that humans were originally nomadic, hunter-gatherers, living on a landmass that was one, single continent. As the sun's path changed from season to season, so would those of the animals that were our food and sustenance, and we would follow, never seeing winter, spring or autumn, always living in the Summerland like one, provident garden of Eden. We walked in the eternal summer, the sun was our mother, our giver of life and our biggest mistake may have been to get tired of walking.

The Bushmen of the Kalahari, noted for their astounding sense of smell, are a really good example of the last vestiges of these nomadic tribes. They were neither patriarchal nor matriarchal, without medicine men or leaders, with everyone, including the children being seen as equal. Their laws for survival, based on love and understanding, included the tribal choice of who was to be allowed to live or die in times of scarcity. This may seem harsh to our modern ways of thinking, but when food could take two weeks to track and catch with water at a premium it was not only necessary but acceptable.

According to Spenser Wells of *The Genographic Project*, the genetic evidence suggests that this tribe may be the oldest in the world with ancestry tracing back to Y-chromosomal Adam, the original man from whom all humans descend. This is not to say that there was only one initial man, or indeed one woman, identified as Mitochondrial Eve. They each would have lived, at different times, in a huge population, but genes on the X and Y chromosomes can be traced back to specific individuals.

The Egyptian Ankh, symbol of life everlasting, has defied explanation, with most Egyptologists locked in an eternal argument about its meaning. However, it may well be a pictorial representation of the sun setting on the horizon that we would have followed day by day, year by year, pointing its way with a navigational cross piece below. Was that perfect sun that was our giver and taker and our solar deity, our very self and therefore symbolic of our own perpetual life in the perpetual sun?

Sir Alan Gardiner went so far as to speculate that the word Ankh may have shared the same spelling as the word sandal, again symbolic of that eternal journey following the sun. Andrew H. Gordon and Calvin W. Schwabe suggest in their book *The Quick and the Dead* that the word ties in to bull, or oxen, again the creatures whose immigrational trails we would have followed and who later would become part of our staple diet. As with any symbol, its meaning is given to it by the people who hold it close to them at the time.

When mankind chose the life of settlement over the life of wandering, the Ankh may well have come to represent a folk memory of the previous life. The sun would no longer have been a constant and the ankh would have come to represent the movement of the sun thought its year and the importance of knowing where and when the sun would be.

This would be the first time that mankind truly encountered winter, cold and death and the need to plot the positioning of settlement. Subsequently the control of a populace fell to the left brain orientated male of the species. No longer could the sun be trusted to come up everyday, as bright and warm as before, and no longer could mankind expect food on his newly invented table. He had to learn about the seasons, and what better way to record that new knowledge than in folk tale passed from mouth to mouth and stone set into the land.

Amongst other things he needed to know was when to plant and grow crops, the timing being dictated not only by the traverse of the no longer perfect solar god through the seasons, but the effect of the moon on the miniature tides within the hoped for seeds of bread. He needed to know when to sacrifice the animals so that enough could survive the winter and enough could be stored to eat though the cold months.

Woman needed to know her cycle, dictated by the moon, for to bring a hungry mouth into a cold and desolate world would be sacrilege and mean certain death. So she ate from the tree of knowledge and truly understood the meaning of procreation and sex, and carried her sacred seed, the genetic bloodline of a line of alpha male rulers, in her revered womb, to give birth at the right time.

Settlement created property and property created jealousy and covertness and the codes were sealed into rock so every man should remember how to live with one another in the cold new world. Archaeologists have shown that the first case of genocide times to man's transition from nomad to settler, when seed and corn, cattle and shelter truly meant the difference between life and death.

And Cain took up his cudgel and murdered his brother, Abel.

So man measured, and wrote down his measurements in story, myth and number so all would remember. He observed the skies, the sun, the moon, the planets, and watched them moving in their not so perfect circles and attempted to map them out for his and his descendants understanding. BUT there was a problem.

Plotting the important times in the year for future memory has always proved tricky because in real terms the earth takes some 365.242190 days to travel around the sun, not a convenient and easy number to remember! Counting may also have seemed like an unsolvable answer to our ancient ancestors, but for the mind-blowing information stored in the genetic material in every cell of our body that causes us to have exactly 10 fingers and 10 toes! It wouldn't matter if we were born with 9 or 8 or 33, we'd have come up with something, but 10 just happens to be the universe given key to decoding its own innermost secrets!

Every culture, since the year dot, has needed a calendar (from the Roman word calare, which means to proclaim), an organized way to note changes of season either written or drawn or mapped out in stones. The Mayans certainly weren't unique in developing their various versions but with a lot of focus on the year 2012 and what has been called the end times, their systems serve to point out the inherent magic in observing the days.

Possibly the first count they developed has been called the Tzolkin count, which comprised 20 weeks of 13 days, 260 days in all. Various explanations have been given for this system, my two favorites being that 260 days is the pregnancy period for humans and cattle and that it takes 260 days to prepare the land ready for planting corn and another 260 days to grow and harvest it. As has already been seen, we have a total of 20 fingers and toes, therefore a great base for counting in, and the number 13 is specifically relevant to the moon as both the amount of lunar months in a year and a quarter of a moons cycle is approximately 7 days – 7 days with 6 nights in between totals 13.

More of this in a minute, the missing 7th night is important!

The second count of the Mayans was called The Haab and was used to mark civil ceremonies and dates. The Haab was made up of 18 months of 20 days each, followed by 5 extra days, known as Uayeb, giving a total cycle length of 365 days. Here we need to stop and pause for thought.

Firstly we have a repetition of our magic number 20, multiplied this time by 18. 18 is 2 times 9, and 9 is 3 squared. To the ancients, the numbers 1 and 2 were often seen as difficult to ratify, 0 was rarely even recognized and the first number with real meaning was 3, because it was a result of the first two, and could be seen in nature as the triad, the first force of true growth, represented by the three fates or goddesses or aspects of god the creator.

But already we have diversified and our thoughts have gone off on a tangent. Numbers were regarded as magical, as were letters, maybe because only the intelligentsia understood them and how to use them and this gave them the power to rule or measure the land, the people and time itself.

What is really amazing is that multiplying 20 by 18 gave the ancients the number 360, a nice clean number that could be counted on the toes and fingers and which was pretty close to the observed number of days in a year.

We are obsessed by linear time, by beginnings and endings and are scared to death of death itself. We will do anything to avoid the natural conclusion of life and events, including creating a whole set of myths and legends to explain it and make it all OK. But this is a misconception installed into our psyches by our own fear and fear mongers who use this for their own means. What the ancients and indeed modern scientists noticed was that everything is circular, in particular the apparent motion of the sun around the earth and that if these 360 days are plotted onto a circle and are used to divide it into arc minutes or degrees then the resulting mathematics and numbers do truly form amazing patterns and codes.

For example, splitting the year into summer and winter splits the 360 days into two sets of 180, that is 10 (the number of fingers) times the magical number 18. Splitting again into quarters to take into account spring and autumn gives us 10 times the magical number 9. Plotting the movement of the planet Venus on this cycle of 360 degrees shows that Venus describes a pentagon as she traverses the skies throughout the year, giving 5 angles of 72 degrees. 7 and 2 add up to the magic number 9 … and so forth. As you can imagine this can pretty much go on forever, and numbers themselves can be made to do anything. However, this is exactly the way early man thought and marked his universe and it worked so well because we are born with 10 fingers and toes!

Already though, this calendar would have been out of sync within a year, so many ancient civilizations, including the Mayans and the Chinese, added a spare 5 days to match to the tropical or solar year. It was these spare days that were often felt to be unlucky, days in which the spirits of the dead could walk the earth and days in which the world might end if the sun didn't reappear to being its next cycle. Of course the number 5 assumed other magical properties, especially with its association with Venus, and here we might start to see why planets were felt to have an influence on our lives and why days were even named after them or their representative spirits or gods.

Back to the Mayan civilization. Many observers believe that there was a conflict between the mathematical and religious calendars and that to attempt to ratify these a third calendar was devised, a combination of both called the calendar round. This consisted of a 52 year cycle of 365 days giving a total of 18,980 days, the smallest number that can be divided evenly by 260 and 365 of the first two calendars. The Mayan's neighbors, the Aztecs, again believed that the end of this cycle spelled the end of the world and were only appeased when the Pleiades crossed the horizon again.

As a result of the Spanish invading America and burning all the Mayans written accounts, only four Mayan documents have been left intact, including one named the *Dresden Codex*. Made from fig-bark that was flattened and covered with a lime paste, it is believed that the 800 or so year old book is a copy of a book made somewhere between the 7th and 9th century AD. It documents various information including astronomical occurrences, rainy seasons and floods mapped against the various Mayan counts including one that has caused the most fuss known as the long count.

The long count seems to have been the Mayans way of recording historical events on a far longer time scale than most other calendars, as is evidenced by its various measures.

In the long count a month or uinal = 20 days or kin.

1 year or tun = 18 uinal = 360 days.
1 katun = 20 tun = 7200 days
1 baktun = 20 katun = 144,000 days (approx 394 years)
Baktun themselves are numbered from 1 to 13. 13 x 144,000 days = 1872000, making a complete cycle just over 5125 years long.

To correlate the long count with the Gregorian calendar, English anthropologist Sir Eric Thompson looked at those Mayan records remaining after the Mexican Inquisition and calculated the beginning of the current Great Cycle as August 13, 3114 B.C. This appears quite strange on first sight as no recorded Mayan date precedes baktun 7, and most of the historical Mayan events occurred during baktun 9 i.e. from 435-830 C.E. However a lot of civilizations seem to set a year dot or founding year for themselves and humanity as only a few thousands years ago, but 3000 B.C. will take on a deeper meaning shortly.

Correlating the long count to the Gregorian calendar also shows, according to some calculations at least, that the next turn of the cycle is around December 2012, hence a general misinterpretation that this must signify the end of the world. But as has already been pointed out the calendar is round, it is cyclic, it begins again and will continue to do so. What would happen if the world ended every 52 years?

Another point of interest regarding the Mayan counting system is that they were one of the first cultures to recognize the number zero and represented it as something looking to me like an egg or seed.

An egg isn't a chicken and a seed isn't corn and yet they both contain the potential for the other. Comparing this, for example, to ancient Hindu belief systems we find the concepts of Maya and Brahma. Maya, the world of form, is actually seen as the world of illusion whilst Brahma, the entirety of creation, contains the blueprints that are the potential for Maya to exist.

The Number 13 and The Moon

It has been observed that the Mayan pyramid in Chichen Itza may have been used as a physical calendar. Each side has a staircase with 91 steps and a platform, for a total of 365 steps. On the Spring and Autumn equinox, at the rising and setting of the sun, the steps at the corner of the north side of the structure can be seen to cast shadows in what appear to be the shape of a serpent - Kukulcan, or Quetzalcoatl. On these two days, the shadows slither down the side of the pyramid with the sun's movement to the carved serpent's head at the base.

The Maya name Chich'en Itza translates as at the mouth of the well of the Itza where chi' means mouth or edge, and ch'e'en, means well. Itzá is the name of the ethnic populous that gained political and economic dominance of the northern peninsula. The name is believed to derive from the Maya itz, meaning magic, and (h)á, meaning water. In the books of the *Chilam Balams* there can be found other, earlier names for this city, Uuc Yabnal, Uuc Hab Nal or Uc Abnal. There is considerable debate about the translation of the second half of these names but most scholars agree that Uuc means seven.

The relevance of the number 7 is born out by a sculpted panel in the Great Ball Court which shows one of the players being decapitated with seven streams of blood spurting from the wound. Six of these become writhing serpents and the middle stream grows into a winding plant.

The 91 steps would seem to symbolize the two numbers 13 and 7, where 13 x 7 = 91 and 13 - 7 = 6. There are 7 days in a lunar week with a remaining 1 ½ representing the dark of the moon. A lot of creation myths have a 7 days week, with sometimes a days rest or completion, additionally they include 7 or even 13 layers of heaven or hell.

Thus the coding in the number 13 can also relate directly to the days in a lunar month with the spare day (7 - 6) telling you to add it on the end for the full round number of days. This way of thinking with floating 1's can be found a lot in ancient mathematics and is found, for example, in creation myths as the 7th day of rest.

As already implied, a calendar based solely on the solar year for growth, planting, animal husbandry etc. would be remiss if it didn't also include the calculations for the phases of the moon as these govern the best times for planting and harvesting crops. Even a few days can matter if there isn't enough food to sustain newborns. Again, compare this train of thought to the social codes of The Bushmen of the Kalahari.

Legend has it that the Emperor Huangdi invented the Chinese calendar back in 2637 B.C.E. Unlike the Islamic calendar, whose months begin when the lunar crescent is first seen after a new moon, or the Jewish calendar, which is moon based but even more complicated, the Chinese month begins on the first day of the new moon when it is in conjunction with the sun and therefore black. The principal term or number of the month is found by observing when the sun's longitude is a multiple of 30 degrees. This is similar to the Indian calendar system, whereby each solar month is defined by the amount of time required for the Sun's apparent longitude to increase by 30 degrees.

Incidentally, in China, the calendar was originally a sacred document, sponsored and circulated by the reigning Emperor, and years used to be counted since the accession of an emperor but are now counted in revolving units of 60. This not only serves to illustrate the deification of the monarch but demonstrates again the link between the King and the land and the universe.

The Measure of Man

This brings us back to two of the recurring numbers in the creation of the calendar, 20 and 13. 20, as has already been mentioned, is the number of fingers and toes, 13 on the other hand, could be the number of major joints in the body, not including fingers and toes - neck, two shoulders, two elbows, two wrists, two hips, two knees and two ankles. So it can be seen that the measure of time links to the proportional measure of man as well as his yearly cycles and the cycles of the universe that affect him and his survival on a day to day basis.

According to Vitruvius, a Roman engineer and architect, writing in the first century CE, the breadth of a man's body, found by measuring from fingertip to fingertip when the hands are outstretched at right angles to the body, is exactly equal to his height, from the soles of his feet to the top of his head, thus forming a perfect square into which both the man's body and the circle that describes it, exactly fits, with his navel being at the exact centre.

With the arms raised and the legs parted, as shown by Leonardo da Vinci, the angle, a measure of ratio and fraction within a circle, becomes critical and since that circle is described by movement then these lengths and angles effectively describe frequency i.e. measurements made over time. This is exactly like the circular calendars of the ancient Mayans.

With respect to both Vitruvius and da Vinci's observations, this fractioning of the human body depicts a number of historically important measurements. The foot for example, the length from heel to toe, is equal to four palms, which is the width of four fingers. A cubit is the width of six palms and is the same length as from the elbow to the tips of the fingers. A yard is three feet and is the distance from the centre of the chest to the outstretched fingers and a fathom is equal to the height and breadth of man, two yards or six feet.

Further more the foot and yard become measures of distance and size, and combining the foot with the circle we find a distinct correlation between the measurement of the foot and the distance of a megalithic yard.

Creating an equilateral triangle, with sides each of a foot long, will generate a circle that has as its radius the distance from the base to the apex of the triangle and as its circumference two megalithic yards. Megalithic yards are the measurements involved in creating megalithic structures, burial mounds and stone circles.

Fascinatingly enough, a lot of work has been done by other authors and mathematicians which not only ties the megalithic mile and yard directly into the circumference of the earth using the value of pi but also its rotational speed, indicating that the perfect foot of exactly 12 inches in length in proportion to the perfect man exactly correlates to the measurement of the planet upon which we live.

Both Leonardo da Vinci and Vitruvius therefore saw the perfect man as directly proportional to his surroundings and the earth itself, and the possibility that megalithic man understood this thousands of years before could be shown by his choice of measurement in the megalithic yard. It is this perfection, not only in ratio but measurement, that produces units that tie into values associated with the measurement of the earth itself, the centre of man's universe.

Building in a time when architecture and measurement was being adopted from these earlier structures informed Vitruvius of the importance, and indeed the sacredness of these measurements. Da Vinci, 1500 years later, was making the same observations about the value of form and ratio expressed in the perfect human body from the perspective of an artist concerned with form and the expression of perfection and therefore beauty. In da Vinci's diagram, man becomes the centre of his own universe with all that he can touch, feel and see being represented by the circle at the end of his fingertips and toes. Conversely though, because Vitruvian man is representative of the measure of the Earth we are able to see the geocentric model within this diagram, where the measure of man and the planet he lives in is contained within the circle and the rest of the universe is mirrored onto the area around the circumference.

Is it possible that the perfect man in the centre of the circle is also man as god, the solar deity Jesus, the son or sun of God? For ourselves we can reinterpret this picture as a representation of the new thought of the golden age that fathered da Vinci, the age of science and recognition, of Galileo and Kepler, where the sun and the earth were put back in their proper place and we can see this picture much like W. E. Hill's copy of the optical illusion featuring a young girl and an old woman. From one viewpoint man is the centre of his universe, the second the earth and yet another the sun or solar deity, the perfect man, and this presents us, with da Vinci's foresight, another code in the making.

In quantum terms, the inside of the circle can be seen as the point at which the multiple probability waves that create the universe collapse into the particles and solids that express its reality, and philosophically the circumference of the circle is the point at which we meet divinity, our higher or subconscious selves that are capable of the process of co-creation. The two spaces are only bound by our imagination, or indeed, lack of it, and the boundary itself is our own, self-created comfort blanket that limits the effect that the uncontrolled manifestation of dreams and nightmares would have on our collective psyches. In effect it stops us staring into the void and facing madness and yet it is also the very same device that can stop our dreams becoming reality.

Extending this thought process back into architecture, a sacred site, space or temple is sacred because it is created on the blueprint of the "perfect" man, which in itself contains the blueprint of the universe and time. Is it no wonder then, that when we are in these temples of the universe, we ourselves enter states of enlightenment, literally feeling as though we are part of creation itself and able to see and be all?

These higher states of being are indeed "perfect" states of being and yet none of us are perfect and are consequently also made more aware of these discrepancies when in these places of power. For some that is true enlightenment, showing them the path to where they "should be" and how to get there, for others it is the opposite and can result in physiological and psychological illness.

In the top of the triangle is the all seeing eye of the perfect man, divinity, the eye of god. There is also the brain, our internal decryption device, which recognizes all sensory input and converts it, like a picture in our head, to our version of reality. If our design is perfect then so is our perception. If however it is modulated by either our own thoughts or external frequency then it is flawed and the geometry of the universe becomes distorted. Hiding beneath the design is the universal glyph of the sun and solar divinity, the dot in the centre of the circle. This not only confirms the identity of the perfect man but verifies the connection of the self to ratio and geometry, manifested for us to see and experience.

Post Script

I recently revisited Castlerigg stone circle in Cumbria, England, a rugged and largely untouched megalithic construction that I haven't visited since my early teens, and lay down amongst the other backpackers and tourists against a stone to take in the beauty of the place. I counted the stones, made a few observations and took my leave. When I got home I thought I would check out a few things on the repository of all knowledge known colloquially as t'internet. I was surprised to find Castlerigg described on various sites as a circle of 38 stones with an inner oblong compound of 10 stones.

For me, standing in the circle at the time and checking an aerial view led me to see a totally different pattern, an outer circle with a second half circle lying against its edge. This second inner circle comprises 13 stones, 3 of which it shares with its parent and yet I seem to be the only commentator that has noticed this! The second semicircle could well be moon shaped, as born out by the number 13, but that's how it felt looking at ground level. The outer circle has 38 stones which together with the outlying kingstone makes 39 i.e. 3x13 where 3 is the number of shared stones.

The maths and geometry of the two lopsided shapes deserve at least a chapter in another tome, but I fell it is safe to say that the pattern is that of two interlocking gears relating directly to the movement of the planets. The same can be seen in the Mayan and Aztec calendar systems where by each circular count can be arranged against the other like a set of gears in order to map out the year by solar, lunar and base 20 variants. Incidentally archaeologists date the construction of Castlerigg to about 3000 BC, the same date the Mayans chose for their year dot!

Together with the da Vinci material and yet more information relating to fractions, quantum mechanics and frequency than can be done justice in this short piece I feel that we can arrive at a number of conclusions.

The most important of these with respect to the code is that man measured the universe according to his own measurements. I believe that he not only identified himself with the universe and the inherent spirit or god of that universe but that he saw its patterns and code, and saw them seemingly striving towards perfection. He modeled his beliefs, myths and spirituality on those patterns, knowing in his heart that he was also a result of those self same patterns. He knew he was one with the land and that because of this oneness he was his own grail, his own message, his own king.

And yet he stopped listening. He believed the stories of his own press officers and fought anyone who disagreed.

And here we are today.

In a land that sings its enchantment to us if we only took time to listen. A land that speaks its magic in patterns and geometry. A land that is truly sacred. A land that is our mother, our God, our king and our code.

Listen to her song.

#

Steve Mitchell - asking questions that modern quantum scientists and archeologists are loath to put on record, such as:

- What is the real purpose and function of stone circles?
- How are they linked to the crop circle and UFO phenomenon?
- Are we alone in the universe or part of a multidimensional matrix with the keys at our fingertips?

With honors degrees in mathematics and music and over twenty years of research and firsthand experience, Steve Mitchell challenges the accepted truth about our ancestors and demonstrates that their wisdom may have been carried into the present day by sacred and quantum science and esoteric lore. A writer and lecturer on mysteries and ancient traditions, his new TV Show, *Mitchell's Wyrd World* and his films *Dragons and Rings* and *Crop Circles – The Enigma* have brought him critical acclaim.

Ancient Code

By Nick Pope

The world now is a very different place to the world I remember as a child. Back then, there were three channels on the TV, the post was delivered twice a day (and coal once a week) and the pocket calculator had yet to be invented. Nowadays we live in a world dominated by gadgets and ways of keeping in touch. Life revolves around laptops, Blackberries, DVDs, i-Pods, FaceBook, Twitter and a seemingly endless list of other so-called conveniences. We ping and poke our way through life, complaining about how little free time we have. Science promised us labor-saving devices that would give us lives of luxury and leisure, yet the irony is that these modern luxuries are the very things that take up so much time. Though not (yet) in a Terminator-style way, we are already slaves to the machines we created. I'm sorry I can't come out, I'm updating my status/installing a new program/configuring my remote control/assembling my flat-pack table - delete as appropriate. We can put a man on the moon, but most major retailers can't even tell you whether they're going to deliver your goods in the morning or the afternoon. All this is called progress, apparently.

But it's not just technology that's changed. We've changed too. Perhaps technology has played a part in this, or perhaps something else is to blame. Gone are the days when people learned a trade from their father or studied hard at a meaningful apprenticeship. We want a quick fix. We're in a rush to get somewhere, even if we're not sure where it is. Children no longer want to be astronauts, firefighters, police officers or nurses. They want to be Big Brother contestants or WAGs.

Does any of this really matter? Hasn't the world just changed, as it always has? I think it does matter, because I think we've lost something important. Because behind issues of ambition and hard work, are deeper issues of identity and self-respect.

Nothing typifies this more than an interview I read with a well-known, old-school manager of a Premiership football club. He was asked why there were so few young English players coming into the game at the highest level. His answer was telling. He explained that when he'd been a child, he and his friends would stay up late, kicking a football around in a warehouse until it got dark, or until the night watchman caught them and kicked them out. He said that this no longer happens in this country. Kids were too busy on their computers and if they played football, it was likely to be a computer game, not the real thing. In Africa and South America, he explained, kids still kick real footballs. That's why there's so much sensational foreign talent coming into our game. Now, that's great for football, but not so good when it comes to selecting an England team, where we can't even find top caliber players to fill all the positions: Google the phrase "left-sided problem" and see what I mean.

Football may seem an odd subject to include in a book like this, but I think the story tells us something very interesting about the modern world, with its quick fix mentality and the erosion of the work ethic. Let me touch on another subject that at first glance might seem odd to include in this book: the ambition of reality TV show contestants. Aside from genre-specific shows where singers want to sing (though don't get me started on singers who don't write their own material and are basically just karaoke singers) or actors who want to act, one hears the same phrase over and over again: "I want to be a TV presenter." It's a fair enough ambition, of course. The problem is that it's often an ambition stated with no real conception of the hard work involved. People think all they have to do is look pretty and chat to pop stars. What could be easier? The reality, of course, is very different. Most times you'll have to keep a lively discussion going about a subject you know nothing about and that bores you senseless. Add to that a guest who dries up, the distraction of a producer talking into your earpiece and various other problems and the truth of the matter is that there's a lot of skill involved if you're to do this well. And unless you're born with a phenomenal gift, the same goes for everything in life. Whether it's a job or a relationship, you need to work at it and you need to work hard.

I realize that this is a very Western view. People all around the world are dying from warfare, malnutrition or preventable disease and despite all my talk of technology, Noam Chomsky has pointed out that the internet is an elite organization and observed that, "Most of the population of the world has never even made a phone call." That may be changing, but is this change for the better? After all, if in the course of my forty four years on this planet I feel we've lost something important, what else have we lost? What truly ancient wisdom is gone? Some things we know about - the library of Alexandria, for example. This is a known unknown. But what about the unknown unknowns? I'm sure readers didn't expect to see this brief essay end with my paraphrasing Donald Rumsfeld. But then, the world is a very strange place.

Nick Pope used to run the British Government's UFO project at the Ministry of Defence. Initially skeptical, his research and investigation into the UFO phenomenon and access to formerly classified government files on the subject soon convinced him that the phenomenon raised important defense and national security issues, especially when the witnesses were military pilots or where UFOs were tracked on radar.

Nick also looked into other mysteries such as alien abductions, crop circles and ghosts. He now continues his research in a private capacity and is recognized as a leading authority on UFOs and the unexplained. He does extensive media work, lectures all around the world and has acted as consultant on numerous television documentaries. www.nickpope.net.

A Glimpse of the Great Beyond?

By Dennis Price
Archaeologist & Author of *Jesus: The Missing Years*

It is frighteningly simple to become seduced by the allure of far-off places, principally because many of us have come to suspect that the hills, deserts, springs or mountains of foreign lands hold some miraculous potential for salvation, or mystical insight, as well as perhaps providing a panacea for our diverse ills. I am as interested as anyone else in exploring certain of the lonely, distant corners of this planet, but my desire to visit these landscapes or monuments stems either from curiosity, or else from an ordinary desire to luxuriate beneath a warm sun while admiring and studying a structure or panorama steeped in antiquity.

I cannot deny that there was a time when I had eyes only for the works of the ancient Egyptians or Mayans, but this was thirty or so years ago, when my sole interest lay in what I perceived to be exotic realms, far removed from the reality of my daily life in the valleys of south Wales. My two children are now equally entranced by what they have seen and read of the world's ancient civilizations, and who can blame them? It is impossible not to marvel at the Seven Wonders of the ancient world, while we would not be human if we were not enthralled by the tales of Odysseus, Sinbad, Marco Polo, Aeneas and Herodotus, to name just a handful of those real and mythical characters whose travels have captivated later generations of readers.

With this in mind, it is understandable that some should yearn to laze on distant, sun-kissed shores, that others should feel the desire to sit at the feet of some mystic in his mountain retreat, that others still should risk the perils of the Boulevard of Broken Dreams on account of their desire for riches and fame in Hollywood, or even that men should die in their hundreds searching for the elusive gold of El Dorado. These ambitions are natural, but there is a malaise that grips us today when we experience intense dissatisfaction with our surroundings, wherever they may be, in the mistaken belief that our immediate locality possesses no value and that only some faraway place or person can fill the emptiness in our souls. To put it another way, "The right path is close at hand, yet Mankind seeks for it afar."

This conviction was bolstered when I first became aware of how many people in Britain take their holidays abroad without having seen more than a fraction of their native land, but I don't doubt that this principle has a universal application. The grass is always greener on the other side, so it follows that we feel a sense of longing and wonderment as we catch an intoxicating glimpse of Paradise on Earth in the form of coral reefs, pyramids, golden sands and exotic shrines, or else we find ourselves drawn to remote wildernesses of snow, rocks, jungle and steppe land. What each destination has in common, whether it be a hulking Scottish castle shrouded in a freezing northern mist or else a Cambodian temple lurking in some humid jungle, is that we more and more suppose that we can find fulfillment in such a location, while we also believe that our thirst for the spiritual, the profound and even the exotic cannot be slaked at home, wherever that may be for each of us.

I should not pretend to be entirely immune from these feelings, because in an ideal world, I would choose to live somewhere in Greece. I first visited one of the many islands back in 1987 and if there is a Heaven on Earth anywhere, then it lies in the close vicinity of the Aegean Sea, to my mind. This is not to disparage any of the other countries of the world, all of which have been blessed with their individual characteristics and qualities that cause others to hold them dear, but I am simply saying that Greece possesses everything my heart could possibly wish for. I could quite happily laze on the beaches, swim in the sea, bask in the sun, eat and drink myself to repletion in the tavernas and wander the scattered ruins until the end of my days in a state of perpetual near bliss. However, as far as spiritual fulfillment is concerned, I have all that I could possibly wish for, and more besides, here among the rolling hills, shady woods and chattering streams of my homeland.

What is the reason for my contentment? Is it because I am privy to some profound secret? Has some revelation been divulged to me by some supernatural being? Have I been vouchsafed a sign?

As far back as I can remember, stories of ghosts or phantoms captured my imagination, undoubtedly because they were glamorous, mysterious and thrilling. As the years passed, I moved on from shivering at tales written especially for children to devouring accounts of real hauntings; I suppose I was beguiled by these strange human or occasionally bestial "things" that seemed to flit tantalizingly in and out of our lives, these "echoes in the darkness" that sometimes evoked feelings of sorrow or sympathy, but which more often inspired fear in those who witnessed their passing.

While I was interested by the individual characteristics of every specter that I heard or read about, wondering what this told me of their nature or purpose, I became more and more fascinated by the ghost stories that had the power to inspire genuine fear, principally those by M.R James. I then discovered the mesmerizing and disturbing works of H.P. Lovecraft, but I was particularly struck by William Hope Hodgson's book *Carnacki the Ghost Finder,* in which the fictional detective Thomas Carnacki made it his business to seek out and render harmless those hauntings or supernatural manifestations that were inimical to human life. Up until that point, I had always understood that hauntings, as opposed to demonic possession or the like, were capable of frightening humans but were incapable of causing harm, so out of pure curiosity I started casting about for any real life examples of such a remarkable phenomenon.

I rapidly learned about many such apparent supernatural manifestations, as these things have been with us since ancient times in the form of the Sirens, but more recently as the Lorelei of the Rhine. The Sirens were not strictly supernatural in origin, but they were nonetheless semi-divine monsters that lured sailors to their deaths, while Pliny the Younger left us a detailed and convincing account of a haunted house in Athens that invariably proved fatal to those who ventured inside the ruins after dark.

I read about other far more recent hauntings with the apparent power to cause harm, such as the house in London's Berkeley Square that acquired a fearful reputation in the 19th century. I regularly heard about dwellings in modern Britain that were said to be infested with poltergeists, but by the time these matters had come to my attention, the supernatural manifestations had either been banished by bell, book and candle, or they had chosen to move on or desist of their own accord. I began to doubt that I would ever have the opportunity of experiencing anything of this nature for myself, but then I remembered the notorious hauntings that were said to be linked with the British barrows, or prehistoric burial mounds.

Once I began to delve into accounts of terrifying manifestations linked with these somber, earthen tumuli, I soon came across other stories of haunted woods, streams, mountains, fields, hills and moors. It rapidly dawned on me that here was a cornucopia of outdoor sites with ominous reputations that had been acquired over the course of centuries or more, while the vast majority of them could be freely visited by anyone caring to brave their alleged terrors without having to seek and acquire permission from a landowner or householder beforehand. So, I soon set out on my first vigil at one of these shunned places and I was astonished by what I discovered there, but I am not planning to regale anyone with ghost stories, even though it is true to say that I have heard, seen and sometimes felt many baffling and disturbing things over the years.

I had been preparing myself for some unpleasant and unnerving experiences at these locations, and this was indeed sometimes the case, but I was astonished by the physical transformation that some of these sites underwent as darkness fell and the cold, distant stars appeared high above me. It was not as if I were in a somber wood one minute, then simply in a darker version of the same place the next, because certain locations acquired a different identity after sunset, even if the same landscape were awash with moonlight, its features as visible as they had been by day.

Furthermore, some of these places were alive, and it is at this point that I find myself groping for words to adequately convey the notion of an animated landscape by night. I visited a remarkable wood in the south of England that was sinister and terrifying, and it is perhaps not difficult for anyone to imagine a place imbued with an oppressive and malevolent atmosphere; as for it being "alive" in any sense, then this came from the feeling that I was constantly being watched, although I cannot say for sure what it was that stared unseen at me from the shadowy depths of the silent trees.

However, this visit was mundane compared to the hours I spent in a supposedly haunted churchyard one night in a remote and sparsely-populated part of England. I had heard lurid yet credible tales of phantoms wandering the locality, so while I was bracing myself for encountering something particularly disconcerting, I was stunned by what eventually manifested itself. After an hour or so of reclining against a crumbling stone wall, peering nervously into the gloom, I became aware that the place was singing, but necessarily to me. I heard no Siren song luring me into a deep pool, no ghostly choir of long-dead monks chanting a thinly-veiled warning to the Ungodly, but the trees and the stones and the glistening stars above combined to produce a melody that seemed to be an affirmation of being and a celebration at the same time. I sensed no enticement, I felt no threat and I could pinpoint no precise spot from which this ethereal chorus emanated, but it happened all the same.

Whatever this unearthly song was, it was mirrored by the stark beauty of the constellations in the night sky, and by the serene yet undoubtedly animated features of the landscape around me. I listened in amazement for a while, then I had to retreat and stumble away through the night because I could no longer physically bear to be in the presence of something of such potency. The overwhelming impression I was left with was that, had I chosen to do so, I could have communed with this "thing," but I was simply fearful that if I had done so, I would have been unprepared for what surely would have followed.

I pondered what had happened that night for years, but while there were many things I was unsure of, I was always certain that I had been blessed by simply being able to undergo such an experience. What it was I was in the presence of, I do not know, but the experience was a spiritual one as opposed to a condition that was merely the by-product of a chance combination of elements, temperature, lighting, mood and evocative surroundings. The other thing that I gradually became aware of, much to my surprise, was that while being in this strange place by night undoubtedly heightened my alertness and possibly my ability to be receptive to things that were out of the ordinary, the hours of darkness were by no means a vital requirement to feeling a genuine connection with something outside my previous experience, or for want of a better expression, something supernatural.

During my time on Salisbury Plain, I came across an entirely ordinary-looking tree overlooking a broad, shallow pool on one of the bends of the river Avon, but when I sat down on one of the huge roots that formed an inviting seat, I found myself at repose in some ancient rural idyll, in a reality far removed from the everyday life I had been in only moments beforehand. There was something benign about the contours of the land and a certain satisfying feel to the wood beneath me, while the reflected sunlight from the water's surface undoubtedly made me feel pleasantly drowsy, but this pleasing effect was not confined to the summer months. This place did not sing to me in the way that the environs of the churchyard to the east had done, but the sensation of communing with something that we do not encounter in the normal course of events was no less dramatic and no less fulfilling.

More recently, as part of writing my book *The Missing Year of Jesus*, I have had renewed cause to visit and investigate particular locations in the West of England and South Wales that possess striking yet hard to define characteristics. Some of these places and their reputations are well known, such as the sublime, peaceful and uplifting atmosphere surrounding Tintagel in Cornwall and the almost tangible aura of sanctity and mystery in Glastonbury. There is also the brooding air of immense antiquity and secrecy that permeates the ruins of Stonehenge, something that draws a million pilgrims a year from around the world to gaze in awe and wonderment at this apparently unfathomable monument, bequeathed to us from remote prehistory.

Much less famous is Nine Barrows Lane in Priddy, in Somerset, the village in which Jesus is said to have worked with the miners in the early years of the first century. Priddy was reputed to have had a "Lord's Walk," which is presumably where Jesus once wandered, but no one now seems to know where this "Lord's Walk" is. Nonetheless, there is a field off Nine Barrows Lane where nine Bronze Age funeral barrows stretch in a gently curving line, and this piece of land possesses an inexplicably serene and restful atmosphere that I have experienced myself, and which others have remarked upon over the years.

I read about Priddy and the field that is home to the nine barrows in literature that is readily available, but as a result of patiently wandering the landscape of the West Country and making polite enquiries of the people who live there, I learned of a stunning location that completely eclipses the rest. I know of no legends whatever that are attached to this curious place, least of all any connected with Jesus, yet it precisely fits the description of one of those places that I am certain that Jesus would have visited, if I am correct in my assertion that this renowned man did indeed spend many years in Britain prior to returning to his homeland to embark upon his famous ministry.

This special place is not hidden by some cloak of invisibility – on the contrary, it is in full, unrestricted view and it is impossible to escape noticing it when you are in the vicinity. In addition to fitting the description of one of those sites to which Jesus would have been drawn while he was in Britain and to which he was most certainly drawn during his ministry, it has other notable qualities such as a silence that is less an absence of sound than a tangible but invisible cloud of sheer serenity.

Whether this astonishing quality is due to one of the world's most spiritual men having once walked and rested there, or whether it is on account of some other cause, either mystical or natural, it is quite simply one of the most uplifting, soothing and enthralling physical locations that I have ever visited. It is almost literally on my doorstep and it took little finding, but I don't doubt that every nation on the face of the planet is home to at least one, if not more, such havens. So, as far as I am able to judge, each and every one of us is perfectly capable of communing with a potent force for good without having to travel to the ends of the Earth to do so. However, I would argue that you do not need to go further than your back garden to discover something truly sublime.

In my book, I have made many references to William Blake, the poet, painter and visionary who wrote the words to *Jerusalem*, which, with its opening line "And did those feet in ancient time walk upon England's mountains green?" is the most famous expression of the legends of Jesus visiting Britain, but Blake also wrote some lines that perfectly capture the notion that "the right path is close at hand ..."

> "To see a World in a Grain of Sand
> And a Heaven in a Wild Flower
> Hold Infinity in the palm of your hand
> And Eternity in an hour."

#

Dennis Price began working on archaeological excavations in the early 1970s in Usk, his home town in South Wales that was formerly the capital of the fearsome Silures tribe. More recently, he became the last archaeologist inside Silbury Hill, Britain's only official pyramid, before work began to seal it off forever in November 2007, but he has also spent years investigating allegedly haunted sites in Britain and abroad, as well as singing in rock bands, working on mediaeval jousting tournaments and appearing in front of the cameras on productions such as *The Crystal Maze*. He runs the Eternal Idol site and his original contributions to the study of Stonehenge and its landscape have been widely reported in the media over the years, but his proudest moment came when the SETI League placed one of his original works alongside others by Sir Arthur C. Clarke. Dennis is the author of *The Missing Years of Jesus – The Greatest Story Never Told* and his favorite film, by a country mile, is *Apocalypse Now*. www.eternalidol.com

Ancient Code

By Colin Wilson

It has long been clear to me that the human animal is trapped in a kind of "worm's-eye view" of reality, like a fly stuck on flypaper, and that most of the literature and philosophy of the past half century has been the buzzing noise it makes in its attempts to escape.

How did this situation arise? The answer lies in a concept I call "the robot," which I formulated about thirty years ago. He is a servant who lives in the brain, and whose job is to facilitate learning. When I learn to type, I have to do it slowly and consciously; then the robot takes over, and does is faster than I could. I learned to ride a bicycle more than sixty years ago. Yet although I have not sat on a bike in years, I could still ride down the road this morning without falling off.

Yet although he is marvelously useful, the robot has one major disadvantage. He not only learns the things I want him to learn, but also things I don't want him to learn. If, for example, I discover a new and delightful country walk, this bloody robot quickly moves in and takes over, so it turns into a mere habit. If I discover an exciting piece of music, he quickly learns it by heart and anticipates every note.

My dog doesn't have this problem. When I take him for a walk, he rushes around in a state of excitement, sniffing every bush. His robot is obviously much simpler than mine. But then he can't talk French or use a computer.

The robot is the main reason that civilization has become a burden to so many of us. As Wordsworth says, "shades of the prison house begin to close" as we grow up and have to learn to cope with its complications.

Yet as soon as we mention prisons, we begin to glimpse an answer to the problem. I know a number of people in prison, and as soon as I think of any of them, it is impossible not to experience, simply by way of contrast, a sense of relief at not being in jail.

One of these acquaintances is an American murderer at present on Death Row, awaiting execution. His name is Danny Rolling, and he is a sex killer. Why did he kill? Because, when in a state of anger about having lost his job, he decided to play Peeping Tom at the house where a pretty girl lived. He had committed rape once in the past – again, when in a state of anger and frustration, but had left the girl alive. This time he decided to break in – although there were two of her male relatives in the house, an uncle and nephew. He tied them at gunpoint, then raped the girl. He was now in a position where he could be identified by three witnesses, and decided he had to kill them. Several more murders followed, including four that caused panic on the University of Florida campus at Gainesville. Caught through DNA profiling, he now awaits execution.

A few evenings ago I saw a program about him on television, and it confirmed the impression that I had received from his letters – that he was a person of considerable intelligence. It was also obvious that he is a man who is bound hand and foot by negative emotions, with their origin in his family.

Then for nearly a decade I corresponded with the "Moors murderer" Ian Brady, until he quarreled over a book I helped him to publish. His accomplice, Myra Hindley, who took part in the murders, is now dead. But again, I felt Brady to be highly intelligent, and that his crimes were a waste of his own life as well as those of his victims. Again, it seemed absurd that anyone would commit crimes that entailed a lifelong loss of freedom.

A third acquaintance at present behind bars is named Ira Einhorn, and I met him in Philadelphia in 1973, when I was teaching there; he was a committed peace activist, who never lost an opportunity to criticize the government. Ira was accused of murdering his girlfriend Holly Maddux when she threatened to leave him. Her body was found hidden in a lumber room in his flat, and Ira claims she was planted there by the CIA in revenge for his years of attacking them. Is it true? I don't know. At first I took Ira's word for it that he had been framed, but the evidence at his trial left me less certain. All I know is that whenever I write to him, I experience a sense of appalling waste of human intelligence.

It was in the 17th century that publishers began issuing accounts of the lives of men who had been condemned to death, and these pamphlets enjoyed a healthy sale before executions. The most famous compilation is called *The Newgate Calendar*, or the *Malefactor's Bloody Register,* and appeared in five volumes in 1760, and is still in print. The reason for their popularity is obvious: because they enabled spectators of executions to focus their relief that they were not on the scaffold. In other words, they created a sensation of freedom. They prevent our robot from taking our freedom for granted – the same sensation I experience when I post a letter to a friend in jail, then take my dog for his afternoon walk.

The German philosopher Fichte put his finger on a central paradox when he remarked, "To be free is nothing; to become free is heavenly." This is because our sense of freedom is quickly neutralized by the robot. What is needed to restore it is a threat to our freedom. Or, less traumatic, to be reminded of it by the arrival of a letter from a friend in prison.

As soon as we think of this situation, its logic becomes obvious. If I had reason to suddenly fear being arrested, the emergency would trigger a flood of adrenalin. If it became apparent that it was all a mistake, I would heave a sigh of relief. This is because the problem has aroused a certain "energy of emergency," and pleasure may be defined as a release of energy – as every child knows when he splashes into a paddling pool on a hot day.

But a moment's consideration shows there is another factor involved - our sense of the reality of the emergency. This has to be the basis of our response. And it could well be the solution of the problem. Graham Greene claims that, as a schoolboy, he played Russian roulette with live bullets to relieve his depression. He had recognized that the answer is to "shake the mind awake."

Consider the nature of the problem which has been stated so vigorously by Philip Gardiner. He can see clearly that it can be summarized in one word: materialism.

What is materialism? It is basically the assumption that we are living in a world of solid, concentrated matter, and that no matter what we do, it is stronger than we are. This belief has been around for more than three centuries, since the time of Galileo, the founder of modern science.

But we should also remember that Galileo and his intellectual contemporaries were not scientists pure and simple. They shared the belief in religion that was part of their age. It was not until the 18th century that a few thinkers arose who thought that religious belief is nonsense. Julien de la Mettrie, who wrote *L'Homme Machine* (Man the Machine) was the first to suggest that man can be defined in purely mechanical terms, and the rage and indignation his book aroused virtually killed him. Even in the "Age of Reason," religious belief was virtually woven into the fabric of the human mind.

Even Darwin, now regarded as the founder of materialistic science, was so worried about the implications of his theory of evolution that he sat on it for two decades, and only decided to publish his conclusions because his contemporary Alfred Russel Wallace had made the same discoveries independently. It also happens that Darwin had ceased to be a Christian as a result of the death of his ten year old daughter Annie in 1851; this emphasizes the fact that Victorian religious belief was basically belief in a benevolent deity who had created a meaningful world.

It would be another 23 years before a young architect named Thomas Hardy produced *Far From the Madding Crowd* in which he clearly stated his belief that human life is governed by chance, which sets in motion the inevitable fate of human beings who mistakenly believe they are free. When a clergyman named Grosart wrote to ask him whether God would be capable of setting evil into motion, Hardy wrote back recommending him to read a life of Darwin.

Hardy's skepticism became part of the underpinning of any self-respecting intellectual in the 20th century. It is, for example, taken for granted by the existentialists of the Second World War. In his novel *L'Etranger* Camus has a story about a sailor who returns to the inn run by his parents, and decides to wait until the next morning to reveal his identity. They murder him in the night for his money. To underline his point, Camus used the same story in a play called *Le Malentendu* (Cross Purposes). He seems to be saying that Hardy's Godless universe has turned actively malevolent.

We do not need to be logicians to recognize that Camus has gone too far. Hardy's universe is indifferent but not hostile. But if we follow Hardy's advice and look to Darwin, we get no closer to an answer to Grosart's question. For Darwin, Natural Selection is another name for chance. And the great problem, as the American philosopher Pierce recognized, is that of "values in a universe of chance." Darwin himself admitted, in *The Descent of Man*, that he was unable to suggest an answer to the question of why zebras have black and white stripes. If they evolved amid trees and bushes it would be easy enough to understand. But in Africa they live in herds on the open savannah.

In *The Occult* I explain my objection to Darwinian selection by mentioning an example I cannot explain: the flattid bug.

In *African Genesis*, Robert Ardrey mentions an example that seems to me a conclusive argument against total, uncompromising Darwinism: the flattid bug. Ardrey was standing with the anthropologist L. B. S. Leakey, looking at a coral-colored blossom like a lilac. Leakey touched the twig, and the flower dissolved into a swarm of tiny insects. A few minutes later the insects resettled on the twig, crawled over one another's backs, and once again became a coral-colored blossom, a flower which does not exist in nature. Some of the insects were green; some were half green and half pink; others were deep coral; they arranged themselves so as to look like a flower with a green tip.

I comment: "Natural selection works in terms of individuals; we cannot imagine a whole colony created by some mass accident of the genes, and then learning to imitate a flower." To explain this, we must assume that the colony has a single intelligent mind.

The naturalist Jeremy Narby has a book called *Intelligence in Nature* in which he examines many similar examples. Its dust jacket says:

"Intelligence in Nature presents overwhelming illustrative evidence that independent intelligence is not unique to humanity alone. Indeed, bacteria, plants, animals, and other forms of nonhuman life display an uncanny penchant for self-deterministic decisions, patterns and actions." One chapter even describes a "smart slime" that can solve a maze.

Narby's quest for intelligence in nature began in 1985 when he went to Peru to study the culture of the Ashaninca Indians, and was told by an old medicine man that the Ashaninca learned about the medicinal properties of thousands of plants by drinking a hallucinogenic brew called ayahuasca, which showed him the answers. His own experience of ayahuasca, described in *The Serpent Power*, was that he was taken over by an intelligence that knew more than he did. He persuaded three scientists to try the experiment, and all three were impressed. (Notably, the two who were totally convinced were women; a male scientist was impressed but found reasons for doubting the experience.)

The archaeologist and researcher Graham Hancock had his own reasons for wanting to explore these realms. He was intrigued by the fact that a basic change seemed to come over mankind about forty thousand years ago, and the result was cave paintings like those of Lascaux and Altamira, portraying ice age mammals and supernatural beings. It was as if our ancestors had suddenly developed paranormal abilities. Is it possible, he wondered, that ancient man suddenly acquired shamistic powers? If so, was the answer that they had stumbled upon ayahuasca or some similar drug – perhaps iboga, known over much of Africa?

He decided to ingest iboga under medical supervision. One effect was to make him feel ill and nauseated. Then the room seemed to fill with a shadowy crowd. Among them he thought he saw his recently deceased father. It seemed he was surrounded by crowds of the dead.

It took him two days to recover from physical weakness and depression. Then he felt renewed. There could be no doubt about the healing power of iboga.

In 2008, he was asked to read a book entitled *Sun of God* by a green campaigner named Gregory Sams. This argues, among other things, that the sun is an intelligent being. What Sams is proposing, says Hancock in his preface, "is that a universal consciousness pervades all matter; whatever its form of existence – that this consciousness is the vibrational DNA of the universe."

His support for the thesis, he agrees, was based on that vision he experienced under iboga: the notion of a spirit reality that lies behind our material universe.

Now it so happens that I had come to this view by a totally different route.

As a child I had become enthusiastic about science: first astronomy, then chemistry, then physics, including relativity and quantum theory. I had every intention of becoming a scientist. But my working class family did not have enough money to send me to university. So when I left school at 16, I had to take a laboring job in a factory while I took my maths exam again, in preparation for taking up an offer to become a laboratory assistant at my old school. I have the factory job, and knew how Dickens must have felt in his blacking factory. As a kind of psychic self-defense I spent all my few time soaking in romantic poetry – Keats, Shelley, Blake. I also became fond of the stories of Hoffmann, and decided I wanted to be a writer. So the lab assistant's job bored me as much as the factory had. I got so depressed I once came close to suicide.

Eventually the school sacked me, and the labor exchange sent me to the office of the Collector of Taxes, a job I stuck until I went into the RAF to do my eighteen months National Service. After a while that bored me as much as the Civil Service, and I "worked my ticket" by claiming to be homosexual (which I am not.) I then decided to become a tramp, and spent that summer wandering around and taking jobs on farms.

All this time I was teaching myself to write by keeping a journal. I began my first novel, based on the Jack the Ripper murders. A marriage to a nurse was unsuccessful and broke up after 18 months. In a department store in my home town I met my present wife Joy, and persuaded her to break off her engagement to a fellow student from Trinity College, Dublin and join me in London. And during that Christmas of 1954, alone in London, I began writing a book I had been thinking of for a long time, a book about "outsiders," social misfits like myself.

At last, my luck changed. It was accepted by a publisher, who gave me a small advance. And when *The Outsider* came out in May 1956, when I was 24, it became a bestseller, and was translated into a dozen or so languages.

The Outsider was basically about the philosophy called Existentialism, and which had been made famous in Paris after the war by Sartre and Camus. You could say that it was about the question of why we are alive, and what we are supposed to do with our lives. Their conclusions, however, were as negative as Thomas Hardy's.

As a teenager I had been deeply impressed by Freud, but by the time I wrote

The Outsider, had come to feel that psychoanalysis was a kind of materialism. The teenage influence of Romanticism had made me detest materialism. It seemed to me that I was fighting a one-man battle against a materialistic civilization. In my teens I had cherished a nostalgia for the Christianity of the Middle Ages, but now I knew this was no solution.

When *The Outsider* came out I was classified with John Osborne and John Braine as an "Angry Young Man." But most of these contemporaries of mine struck me as brainless. Now it seemed to me that I had no true contemporaries, no true allies. I had to remain an "outsider" whether I liked it or not.

The remaining half dozen books of my *Outsider* cycle continued to deal with what interested me most: consciousness and the imagination – in other words, they remained preoccupied with the philosophy of Existentialism. The most important discovery I stumbled upon during the decade I devoted to these books was the work of the philosopher Edmund Husserl, the creator of the philosophy called Phenomenology, which became the foundation of modern Existentialism.

Quite simply, Husserl's great discovery was that in order to perceive anything, you have to fire your attention at it as an archer fires an arrow at a target. If you look at your watch without this kind of attention, you do not notice the time, and have to look again. Husserl called this faculty "intentionality," and it is what consciousness is intended for, just as your hands are intended for grasping. Without the use of this faculty, reality appears somehow unreal. And for me, this explained why so many of the Romantics has committed suicide.

But after a book called *Introduction to the New Existentialism* (1967), my work suddenly took a totally new direction.

In the autumn of 1969, my American agent asked me if I would be willing to write a book about "the occult" for the New York publisher Random House. It was not a subject that interested me deeply, for although I had read books on spiritualism and hauntings in my childhood, my subsequent passion for science had made me decide it was all nonsense and wishful thinking. Nevertheless, I accepted the commission to keep my bank manager happy, convinced that it would involve telling absurd tales of ghosts with their heads underneath their arms, and prepared to write with my tongue in my cheek.

In fact, the subject soon had me fascinated. My wife Joy happened to be reading Osbert Sitwell's autobiography *Left Hand, Right Hand*, which described how, just before the beginning of the First World War, he and a group of brother officers had gone to visit a celebrated palmist. She looked more and more worried as she read their hands. When one of them took her aside and asked what was the matter, she said: "I could see nothing in their hands." A few months later the war broke out, and most of them were killed.

Then I read Robert Graves's *White Goddess,* with its argument that there are two kinds of knowledge, "lunar" and "solar." Solar knowledge is the kind of rational, "daylight" knowledge that is the foundation of our technological civilization. Lunar knowledge is an older kind which rises from depths of intuition. I met Graves when I was in Majorca, and was impressed with his conviction that there is a kind of knowledge that somehow "leaps" straight from question to answer, without the benefit of intervening stages. And the more I read about "second sight," ghosts, telepathy and precognition, the more I realized that modern civilization has forgotten a whole dimension of consciousness that once came naturally to tribal shamans, and that we shall remain trapped in a kind of mental dungeon unless we can regain it. In fact, I realized that our dream of a purely rational science is a delusion, and that we shall have to learn to recapture lunar knowledge.

To my astonishment, *The Occult* (1971) became a bestseller in England and America, although there were many people who reproached me with "selling out" to the current fad for anti-rationalism, and argued that I was "selling human nature short." I replied that I had been fighting the battle against rationalism since I wrote my first book *The Outsider* in 1955, and felt that if paranormal powers like precognition and telepathy really exist, then it is the pessimists and rationalists who have been "selling human nature short."

As a result of my burgeoning interest in the paranormal, I went on to write two sequels to *The Occult* – *Mysteries* and *Beyond the Occult,* and even allowed myself to be persuaded to go to Pontefract, in Yorkshire, to look into a case of a poltergeist haunting. This left me totally convinced that poltergeists – "banging ghosts" – are not some kind of manifestation of the unconscious minds of adolescents, but are, in fact, "spirits." Until then, I had not believed in ghosts – or rather, had kept an open mind about them – but this new insight left me in no doubt of their reality.

What effect did this have on my interest in philosophy? Quite simply, the same effect that the experience of ayahuasca had on Jeremy Narby, or iboga on Graham Hancock. It made me aware of a realm of reality behind the everyday, material face of existence. In other words, "existentialism" became for me a far wider category.

Now until the late 1960s, I had considered myself a kind of "existentialist" philosopher, who was attempting to rescue existentialism from the pessimism of Sartre, Camus, and Heidegger. But after the request from Random House, I began to give the matter some new thought, and began to ask people of my acquaintance whether they had ever had any "paranormal" experiences. I was surprised by the number who said yes.

One friend was a concert pianist called Mark Bredin. He told me how he had been returning, very late at night, from a concert in central London, and traveling in a taxi along the Bayswater Road. Suddenly, he knew with absolute certainty that the next traffic light, a taxi would try to "jump" the light, and would hit them sideways. He wondered if he ought to warn his driver, but felt that he might be regarded as slightly mad. And at the next traffic light, a taxi tried to "beat" the light at Queensway and hit them sideways.

What peculiar power could make Mark aware of something that would happen in the future? I had already recognized that the mind possesses the power to escape from pessimism and defeat by meditating on a sudden emergency, like Dostoevsky awaiting death in front of a firing squad. But this was something altogether more strange and unusual.

Another friend, the historian A. L. Rowse, told me how he had been leaning out of a window in Oxford. The window frame was very heavy, and it occurred to him that if it fell, it might easily kill him. Since he was in a bad mood, he thought: "Let the damn thing fall!" A few moments later, just after he had withdrawn his head, the window fell.

Rowse also told me how, one quiet afternoon, he had a sudden premonition that if he went into the college library, he would find two young men embracing. He crossed two quadrangles and walked into the library—and saw the two young men embracing.

Even odder was an experience described to me by a middle-aged friend named Kay Lunnis, who spent several days a week in our house, helping to look after our children. Kay described how she had once been seriously ill, and had felt herself rise up above her body so she could look down on it; then she had descended and re-entered her body.

A few years earlier I would have at least considered the possibility that this was some kind of hallucination due to fever. But in gathering material for *The Occult*, I had come across far too many cases of "out-of-the-body experiences" to doubt that it was possible. Another friend, Lyall Watson, had described how, when his vehicle overturned in Kenya, he suddenly found himself hovering above the bus, and looking at the head and shoulders of a boy who had been hurled halfway through the canvas roof. It occurred to him that if the bus rolled any further, the boy would be crushed. A few minutes later, he recovered consciousness in the driving seat, got out of the vehicle, and rescued the boy, who was in exactly the position he had seen a few moments earlier.

Now, if these friends were telling the truth—and I was strongly inclined to believe that they were - then human beings possess at least two faculties that were unsuspected by materialists like Heraclitus, Schopenhauer, and Samuel Beckett: the power to "see" the future, and the power to "leave the body."

Now quite clearly, if this were true, then it should be taken into account in any attempt to create a "philosophy of human existence." Such a philosophy demands that we try to understand "what man is." And if, in certain moments, man can see into the future, then he is certainly more than philosophers had assumed.

Inevitably, I also had to reconsider the question of life after death. Another friend, Professor G. Wilson Knight, was a convinced spiritualist, and told me a circumstantial story that seemed to prove beyond all doubt that his mother had survived death. Now Dostoevsky had once remarked that if there is such a thing as life after death, it would be the most important thing that human beings could possibly know. And Dostoevsky was the most profound of the "existential" philosophers. In *The Brothers Karamazov*, Ivan Karamazov argues that the world is so full of suffering that no "religion" can justify it; Ivan says that he wants to "give God back his entrance ticket." Here he is expressing the philosophy of Heraclitus and Ecclesiastes and Sartre - that in a world dominated by brute matter, man is a useless passion who is doomed to defeat. Yet Dostoevsky recognized that if there is life after death, this fact would change everything.

This, then, is why I regarded the evidence of the paranormal as so important. According to modern Western philosophy, which begins with Descartes, it is the philosopher's duty to "doubt everything" until he has achieved a residue of ultimate certainty—no matter how small—on which he can take his stand. Unfortunately, this method has failed to yield any kind of certainty. It led Bishop Berkeley to doubt the existence of the material world and David Hume to doubt cause and effect, and even the existence of the "self." It led Sartre to conclude that "it is meaningless that we live and meaningless that we die," and Camus to regard human life as "absurd." The most fashionable of modem French philosophers, Jacques Derrida, is quite simply a descendant of Heraclitus, who believes that there is no such thing as "underlying meaning" (which he calls "presence") in the universe; the only reality is the endless flux of matter.

Yet as soon as we begin to study the paranormal, we immediately encounter the existence of all kinds of powers that contradict materialism. Far from being a mere reflection on the surface of a pond, man seems to be like an iceberg whose most important part is hidden below the surface. Of course, Freud and Jung had already told us about the unconscious. But it would seem that even they underestimated its powers. Even the anecdotes I have recounted above seem to indicate that the part of the self hidden below the water-line possesses virtually magical powers.

And of course - as Dostoevsky recognized - the ultimate contradiction of the view that we possess "no self" would be an actual proof of life after death, for without a self, there would be nothing to survive death. This ultimate proof eludes us; but the existence of other paranormal powers seems to leave no doubt of the truth of the "iceberg" view of the human mind.

Moreover, it seems clear that some of these powers that lie below the surface seem to contradict the "scientific" view of man. Science tells us that the future has not yet happened; therefore we can only guess what is going to happen. Yet when he was deeply relaxed, Mark Bredin had a clear premonition of what would happen when his taxi reached the next traffic light.

As I thought about these unknown faculties, I remembered another strange insight I had stumbled on a few yeas ago.

In 1843, an archaeologist named Botta had discovered in the ancient library of King Assurbanipal (669-626 BC) in Nineveh a clay tablet containing a vast number, 195,955,200,000,000. It baffled both archaeologists and scientists. Using a computer, a space engineer named Maurice Chatelain discovered that this number is 60 multiplied by 70 to the power of seven.

Recalling that the ancient Sumerians, who did their counting in sixties rather than tens, he wondered if the Nineveh number might be in seconds, and worked it out to be something over six million years.

Now in astronomy there is an important cycle known as the processional cycle. The equinoxes "precess" (go backwards), and take just under 26,000 years to get back to their starting point. Chatelain tried dividing this into the Nineveh number, and discovered it divided precisely 240 times.

Now he found himself wondering if this giant number might be what astrologers and occultists used to refer to as "the great constant of the solar system," a "highest common factor" into which all other numbers - planetary orbits, and so on - will divide. He proceeded to calculate the cycles of the planets and their satellites in seconds, and found that each would divide exactly into the Nineveh number.

This was a staggering discovery. Modern science assumes that these ancient astronomers were interested in the heavens for purely superstitious reasons. But if the Nineveh number was what it was supposed to be, it proved that the Chaldean astronomers understood our solar system as well as Isaac Newton did.

To test his result still further, Chatelain compared the period of the earth's rotation with the figure obtained from the Nineveh number. He was slightly puzzled to find a slight discrepancy in the sixth decimal place. Admittedly, this was only a twelve-millionth of a day per year. But the Nineveh number had so far proved itself so accurate that he could not understand even such a tiny difference.

Then it dawned on him. We now know that the earth is slowing down very slowly. It will take twelve million years before a year is even a day shorter.

For the Nineveh number to fit our earth's rotation with total accuracy, you have to assume that it was calculated 64,800 years ago.

That sounds absurd. Surely there were no intelligent beings around that long ago?

According to the Nineveh number, there must have been.

Who were they? One guess is that they were our early ancestors, Cro-Magnon man. Another, I have suggested, is his predecessor Neanderthal Man.

Clearly, these ancient astronomers possessed a greater knowledge of the heavens than most of their modern colleagues.

Now I recalled that my old friend John Michell, author of *The View Over Atlantis,* believed the ancients possessed an amazing number lore, and wrote to him to ask if he could throw any light on the Nineveh number. He could. He pointed out to me that the number is also divisible by the diameter of the sun (864,000 miles) and of the moon (2160 miles). He also suggested I read a chapter in his book *The Dimensions of Paradise* about the knowledge of astronomy possessed by the ancients. I did, and it staggered me.

He shows, to begin with, that the circumference of the moon, the earth, the sun, the moon's orbit around the earth, and the earth's orbit around the sun, can be divided precisely by twelve to the power of seven, and concludes that ancient philosophers "established that number in feet as the measure of the moon's circumference, and made it the astronomical standard measure of the universe."

I began to see what he meant in his accompanying letter by the statement: "We are dealing here with an entire, organic cosmic code of number which structures the universe, not just odd coincidences."

What does it all mean? Well, to begin with, you could say that our ancestors of long ago apparently knew far more than we give them credit for.

Let me return to the question I raised at the beginning of this piece: how modern man has become trapped in a "worm's eye view," like a fly on sticky fly paper.

A few weeks ago I came upon a review of a film called *No Country for Old Men*, which had been considered for many Academy Awards. It was brutal, the reviewer conceded, but the author, Cormac McCarthy, might well deserve the Nobel Prize. When I saw that it was being shown on television I recorded and watched it. It was so obscure that I found it impossible to follow, so I purchased the novel. This proved equally obscure and equally brutal, with an assassin trying to hunt down a man who has found a briefcase with two million dollars from a drug deal gone wrong. The sheriff who narrates much of the book admits that he finds the modern world too brutal for him ("No country for old men") and proposes to retire.

I found another book by McCarthy called *The Road*, about an old man and a boy walking through a landscape devastated by nuclear war. I soon gave this up.

Why, I wondered, is a man who is being tipped for the Nobel Prize writing works as negative as this?

Well, I suppose it's a logical extension of the mood of Camus or Beckett. We have seen how this came about, from the exhausted Romanticism of the 19th century, which began with such extraordinary hopes for the human race – "Bliss was it in that dawn to be alive," said Wordsworth – yet by 1830 had collapsed into misery. No wonder Yeats called the late Romantics "the tragic generation."

But before we swallow that answer, we should at least ask whether the tragedy was inevitable. And Yeats's career seems to suggest that it was not. He survived the wreckage and went to turn himself into a great poet. As we look at those tragic "Outsiders" of the 19th century, as I did in my first book, it becomes clear that most of them were responsible for their own defeat; it was born out of their own pessimism and self-pity.

The source of that pessimism may be pinned down in the work of the Scottish philosopher David Hume, who in his *Treatise of Human Nature* (1739) denied that we possess a "self." "When I enter most intimately into what I call myself, I always stumble on some particular perception or other … I never catch myself at any time."

How is it possible for a normal person to conclude that he has no self? Well, it is not difficult if you feel tired or depressed - teenagers are rather prone to it. In that mood you feel you are reacting passively to whatever life throws at you. And life seems to make sure that these are the times when you feel a cold coming on, or the larger-than expected electricity bill arrives …

Less than a decade after Hume's Treatise, *La Mettrie's Man the Machine* was published (1748). And by the end of that century, the view that man is a machine was widely accepted by most French intellectuals.

I should add that the hidden motive behind this was a revolt against the Catholic Church, and its dogmas and intellectual tyranny. So I've always had a good deal of sympathy for La Mettrie. He was followed by Condillac and Cabanis. Condillac arguing that our so-called mental life is merely a matter of physical sensations, and Cabanis that the brain secretes thoughts as the liver secretes bile.

But for me, the first of the great "positive psychologists" - psychologists who recognized the reality of the self - was another Frenchman, Maine de Biran, who flourished around the beginning of the 19th century. He was a soldier who retired to a castle in the Dordogne to devote his life to philosophy. Although he started off as a follower of Condillac, he gradually became more and more opposed to this idea that man is nothing more than a penny in the slot machine. He pointed out that when I'm making some kind of real effort, I have a clear feeling that it is I who am doing it, not a machine. I may feel mechanical when I'm doing something boring and automatic, but as soon as I exert my will, I become aware that I'm not a machine - that I possess an "active power."

This vital insight could have altered the course of French philosophy, but no one was really interested in pursuing the idea that man possesses free will. It probably struck these philosophers as an attempt to let in religion by the back door.

Immediately after Maine de Biran, the most influential philosophy was

Auguste Comte, who created what he called his "positive philosophy." He thought that the basic trouble with human beings is false belief - superstition - which includes every form of religion, and that once man has turned his back on the superstition, we shall suddenly have a race of truly free human beings.

Unfortunately, French philosophy - and English philosophy - pursued this more or less mechanistic line of Condillac and Comte, and it was developed in England by John Stuart Mill, and later by Herbert Spencer. And of course, then Freud came along, and although he deeply shocked the late Victorians, his philosophy was really, in fact, as mechanistic as Condillac's. Man is nothing more than a helpless puppet in the hands of his unconscious mind, over which he has no power whatever. Freud recognized that this philosophy was deeply pessimistic, but said, that, unfortunately was the truth about the universe, and we had to accept it.

In fact, the next great "positive psychologist" after Maine de Biran was William James, who began to believe in the importance of free will as a result of an appalling experience which almost cost him his sanity. As a young man who had received a brilliant education, James suddenly found himself in the position of not knowing where he wanted to go or what he wanted to do. This feeling of total uncertainty about yourself and your future can easily lead to a kind of inner collapse. Man actually recharges his vital batteries by the activity of his will, and if this activity ceases as a result of pessimism or total lack of purpose, he begins to run down. He falls into the hands of his "robot."

James goes on to describe how, in this state of low vitality and self doubt, he went into a room at twilight, when there suddenly appeared to his mind's eye the image of an idiot he had seen recently in a mental home. This man had a greenish face and long black hair and was staring blankly in front of him. James suddenly had the horrifying thought: "If the hour should strike for me as it struck for him, nothing I could do could possibly save me from his fate." He said that it was his sudden perception of the merely momentary discrepancy between himself and the idiot that filled him with horror, and caused a kind of inner collapse. From then on, he went around in a state of deep misery, totally convinced that he could do nothing of any importance.

He also became totally convinced that Condillac was right, and that man is merely a machine. Everything we do is directed by some motive, and can therefore be regarded as mechanical.

This thought depressed him profoundly, until one day he read the work of a French philosopher called Charles Renouvier, who remarked that, although most of the things we do can be explained in purely mechanical terms, there is one thing which obviously demonstrated our free will: we can think one thought rather than another. And as James thought about this, it suddenly struck him that this is obviously true. You can change the direction of your thoughts as often as you like. This totally convinced James of the reality of free will, and from that moment onwards, he began to recover his mental balance and sense of health.

This, then, explains what went wrong with western culture nearly three centuries ago, and why literature has fallen into the hands of the Becketts and McCarthys.

How could it be reversed? Here the cheering news is that it is already happening. The reaction against Freud began with Jung's recognition that "the soul possesses a religious function." The American Abraham Maslow complained that Freud has "sold human nature short," and proposed a new psychology based upon the "peak experience," those moments that Chesterton called "absurd good news." Another American named George Pransky has set about creating a "renaissance in psychology" based upon the insights of a remarkable mystic, Syd Banks, Pransky writes: "At this point, a friend from Vancouver Island told him that he had discovered an extraordinary teacher called Syd Banks. "Two years prior," says Pransky, "Mr. Banks experienced an epiphany that was of such magnitude that he was scarcely recognizable as the person he was before the experience. From a few seconds of revelation and the resultant two days of revelation from that experience, Syd Banks was transformed from a shy, insecure person to a person of uncommon well-being, vitality and wisdom … Here was a man with a pre-grammar school education who previously had difficulty giving a toast at a party of friends who was now comfortable sharing his new-found knowledge with people with advanced degrees."

What had happened was this. Walking with a friend, Syd Banks had remarked: "I'm so unhappy," and his friend had replied: "You're not unhappy, Syd, you just think you are." This was the revelation that transformed Syd Banks's life. It was the recognition that we create most of our unhappiness through our negative thoughts.

The phrase I find most significant in Pransky account is "and the resultant two days of revelation." The insight had to unfold in his mind until he grasped its full significance. And that significance was the realization that we are all the time creating problems that do not exist.

A final note: this has been recognized for at least two thousand years. The philosopher Epictetus lived some time after 50 AD, and was a Stoic - at one time a Roman slave, who was given his freedom. It was Epictetus who encapsulated the discoveries of Syd Banks when he said: "What alarms and disturbs man are not real things, but his opinions and fancies about things."

# # #

Born and raised in Leicester in England (U.K.), Colin Wilson left school at 16, worked in factories and at various occupations, and read in his spare time. When Wilson was 24, Gollancz published *The Outsider* (1956) which examines the role of the social "outsider" in seminal works of various key literary and cultural figures. These include Albert Camus, Jean-Paul Sartre, Ernest Hemingway, Hermann Hesse, Fyodor Dostoyevsky, William James, T. E. Lawrence, Vaslav Nijinsky and Vincent Van Gogh and Wilson discusses his perception of Social alienation in their work. The book was a bestseller and helped popularize existentialism in Britain. Critical praise though, proved short-lived, and Wilson was soon widely criticized.

Literary critics labeled Wilson an Angry Young Man. He contributed to *Declaration*, an anthology of manifestos by writers associated with the movement, and a popular paperback sampler, *Protest: The Beat Generation and the Angry Young Men*, excerpted a chapter of *The Outsider*. Wilson and his friends Bill Hopkins and Stuart Holroyd, were viewed as a sub-group of the "Angries" that was more concerned with "religious values", than liberal or socialist politics. Critics on the left swiftly labeled them as fascistic; commentator Kenneth Allsop called them "the law givers."

Wilson's works after *The Outsider* focused on positive aspects of human psychology, such as peak experiences and the narrowness of consciousness. He admired the humanistic psychologist Abraham Maslow and corresponded with him. Wilson wrote *The War Against Sleep: The Philosophy of Gurdjieff* on the life, work and philosophy of G. I. Gurdjieff — an accessible introduction to the Greek-Armenian mystic in 1980. He argues throughout his work that the existentialist focus on defeat or nausea provides only a partial representation of reality and that there is no particular reason for accepting it. Wilson views normal, everyday consciousness buffeted by the moment, as "blinkered" and argues that it should not be accepted as showing us the truth about reality. This blinkering has some evolutionary advantages in that it stops us from being completely immersed in wonder, or in the huge stream of events, and hence unable to act. However, to live properly we need to access more than this everyday consciousness.

www.ingramcontent.com/pod-product-compliance
Lightning Source LLC
Chambersburg PA
CBHW061301110426
42742CB00012BA/2007